Capital Punishment
Second Edition

Capital Punishment

Second Edition

Alan Marzilli

SERIES CONSULTING EDITOR
Alan Marzilli, M.A., J.D.

CHELSEA HOUSE
PUBLISHERS
An imprint of Infobase Publishing

Capital Punishment, Second Edition

Copyright © 2008 by Infobase Publishing

Chelsea House
An imprint of Infobase Publishing
132 West 31st Street
New York NY 10001

Library of Congress Cataloging-in-Publication Data

Marzilli, Alan.
  Capital punishment / Alan Marzilli. — 2nd ed.
    p. cm. — (Point/Counterpoint)
  Includes bibliographical references and index.
  ISBN 978-0-7910-9796-0 (hardcover)
  1. Capital punishment—Juvenile literature. I. Title. II. Series.

HV8694.M327 2008
  364.66—dc22   2008002976

Chelsea House books are available at special discounts when purchased in bulk
quantities for businesses, associations, institutions, or sales promotions. Please call
our Special Sales Department in New York at (212) 967–8800 or (800) 322–8755.

You can find Chelsea House on the World Wide Web at
http://www.chelseahouse.com

Series design by Keith Trego and Erik Lindstrom
Cover design by Keith Trego and Ben Peterson

Printed in the United States of America

Bang NMSG 10 9 8 7 6 5 4 3 2 1

This book is printed on acid-free paper.

All links and Web addresses were checked and verified to be correct at the time of
publication. Because of the dynamic nature of the Web, some addresses and links
may have changed since publication and may no longer be valid.

FOREWORD

Alan Marzilli, M.A., J.D.
Washington, D.C.

The POINT/COUNTERPOINT series offers the reader a greater under-standing of some of the most controversial issues in contemporary American society—issues such as capital punishment, immigration, gay rights, and gun control. We have looked for the most contem-porary issues and have included topics—such as the controversies surrounding "blogging"—that we could not have imagined when the series began.

In each volume, the author has selected an issue of particular importance and set out some of the key arguments on both sides of the issue. Why study both sides of the debate? Maybe you have yet to make up your mind on an issue, and the arguments presented in the book will help you to form an opinion. More likely, however, you will already have an opinion on many of the issues covered by the series. There is always the chance that you will change your opinion after reading the arguments for the other side. But even if you are firmly committed to an issue—for example, school prayer or animal rights—reading both sides of the argument will help you to become a more effective advo-cate for your cause. By gaining an understanding of opposing argu-ments, you can develop answers to those arguments.

Perhaps more importantly, listening to the other side sometimes helps you see your opponent's arguments in a more human way. For example, Sister Helen Prejean, one of the nation's most visible oppo-nents of capital punishment, has been deeply affected by her interac-tions with the families of murder victims. By seeing the families' grief and pain, she understands much better why people support the death penalty, and she is able to carry out her advocacy with a greater sensi-tivity to the needs and beliefs of death penalty supporters.

The books in the series include numerous features that help the reader to gain a greater understanding of the issues. Real-life examples illustrate the human side of the issues. Each chapter also includes excerpts from relevant laws, court cases, and other material, which provide a better foundation for understanding the arguments. The volumes contain citations to relevant sources of law and information, and an appendix guides the reader through the basics of legal research, both on the Internet and in the library. Today, through free Web sites, it is easy to access legal documents, and these books might give you ideas for your own research.

Studying the issues covered by the Point-Counterpoint series is more than an academic activity. The issues described in the book affect all of us as citizens. They are the issues that today's leaders debate and tomorrow's leaders will decide. While all of the issues covered in the Point-Counterpoint series are controversial today, and will remain so for the foreseeable future, it is entirely possible that the reader might one day play a central role in resolving the debate. Today it might seem that some debates—such as capital punishment and abortion—will never be resolved.

However, our nation's history is full of debates that seemed as though they never would be resolved, and many of the issues are now well settled—at least on the surface. In the nineteenth century, abolitionists met with widespread resistance to their efforts to end slavery. Ultimately, the controversy threatened the union, leading to the Civil War between the northern and southern states. Today, while a public debate over the merits of slavery would be unthinkable, racism persists in many aspects of society.

Similarly, today nobody questions women's right to vote. Yet at the beginning of the twentieth century, suffragists fought public battles for women's voting rights, and it was not until the passage of the Nineteenth Amendment in 1920 that the legal right of women to vote was established nationwide.

What makes an issue controversial? Often, controversies arise when most people agree that there is a problem, but people disagree about the best way to solve the problem. There is little argument that poverty is a major problem in the United States, especially in inner cities and rural areas. Yet, people disagree vehemently about the best way to address the problem. To some, the answer is social programs, such as welfare, food stamps, and public housing. However, many argue that such subsidies encourage dependence on government benefits while unfairly penalizing those who work and pay taxes, and that the real solution is to require people to support themselves.

American society is in a constant state of change, and sometimes modern practices clash with what many consider to be "traditional values," which are often rooted in conservative political views or religious beliefs. Many blame high crime rates, and problems such as poverty, illiteracy, and drug use on the breakdown of the traditional family structure of a married mother and father raising their children. Since the "sexual revolution" of the 1960s and 1970s, sparked in part by the widespread availability of the birth control pill, marriage rates have declined, and the number of children born outside of marriage has increased. The sexual revolution led to controversies over birth control, sex education, and other issues, most prominently abortion. Similarly, the gay rights movement has been challenged as a threat to traditional values. While many gay men and lesbians want to have the same right to marry and raise families as heterosexuals, many politicians and others have challenged gay marriage and adoption as a threat to American society.

Sometimes, new technology raises issues that we have never faced before, and society disagrees about the best solution. Are people free to swap music online, or does this violate the copyright laws that protect songwriters and musicians' ownership of the music that they create? Should scientists use "genetic engineering" to create new crops that are resistant to disease and pests and produce more food, or is it too risky to use a laboratory to create plants that nature never intended? Modern medicine has continued to increase the average lifespan—which is now 77 years, up from under 50 years at the beginning of the twentieth century—but many people are now choosing to die in comfort rather than living with painful ailments in their later years. For doctors, this presents an ethical dilemma: should they allow their patients to die? Should they assist patients in ending their own lives painlessly?

Perhaps the most controversial issues are those that implicate a Constitutional right. The Bill of Rights—the first 10 Amendments to the U.S. Constitution—spell out some of the most fundamental rights that distinguish our democracy from other nations with fewer freedoms. However, the sparsely-worded document is open to interpretation, with each side saying that the Constitution is on their side. The Bill of Rights was meant to protect individual liberties; however, the needs of some individuals clash with society's needs. Thus, the Constitution often serves as a battleground between individuals and government officials seeking to protect society in some way. The First Amendment's guarantee of "freedom of speech" leads to some very difficult questions. Some forms of expression—such as burning an American flag—lead to public outrage, but are protected by the First Amendment. Other types of expression that most people find objectionable—such as child pornography—are not protected by the Constitution. The question is not only where to draw the line, but whether drawing lines around constitutional rights threatens our liberty.

The Bill of Rights raises many other questions about individual rights and societal "good." Is a prayer before a high school football game an "establishment of religion" prohibited by the First Amendment? Does the Second Amendment's promise of "the right to bear arms" include concealed handguns? Does stopping and frisking someone standing on a known drug corner constitute "unreasonable search and seizure" in violation of the Fourth Amendment? Although the U.S. Supreme Court has the ultimate authority in interpreting the U.S. Constitution, their answers do not always satisfy the public. When a group of nine people—sometimes by a five-to-four vote—makes a decision that affects hundreds of millions of others, public outcry can be expected. For example, the Supreme Court's 1973 ruling in *Roe v. Wade* that abortion is protected by the Constitution did little to quell the debate over abortion.

Whatever the root of the controversy, the books in the Point-Counterpoint series seek to explain to the reader both the origins of the debate, the current state of the law, and the arguments on either side of the debate. Our hope in creating this series is that the reader will be better informed about the issues facing not only our politicians, but all of our nation's citizens, and become more actively involved in resolving these debates, as voters, concerned citizens, journalists, or maybe even elected officials.

What Is Capital Punishment?

S ome of today's greatest moral and legal questions concern capital punishment. Should the government have the power to sentence convicted criminals to death? Throughout history, societies have punished criminals by executing them, but today many nations have abolished the death penalty. In the United States, however, the federal government and many individual states continue to sentence people to death.

A Brief History of Capital Punishment

In ancient times, methods of execution were particularly bloody. In addition to crucifixion, the Bible mentions punishments such as stoning, which meant being put to death by a crowd of people throwing stones. The death penalty was given for crimes that would be considered minor, or not crimes at all, by today's standards. For centuries—throughout the Middle Ages and the Renaissance—little changed. According to Harry Henderson:

> Death was the standard penalty for major crimes across Europe. The methods of execution used frequently were cruel and barbaric by modern standards, often involving some form of torture. The condemned were subject to such ordeals as burning at the stake, being broken on a wheel, or being crushed under heavy stones.[1]

The first significant effort to make executions more humane occurred during the French Revolution of 1789. Prior to the revolution, members of the aristocracy were executed swiftly by sword. By contrast, peasants and laborers were executed by the slow, torturous methods common at the time. Physician Joseph-Ignace Guillotin proposed to the French Assembly that, in the interest of fairness and equity upon which the Revolution was based, like crimes should be punished with like penalties, and all people put to death should be punished by the same method. He suggested the use of a machine that would behead a condemned person by means of a heavy blade that dropped swiftly onto the back of the neck. This device, eventually called a guillotine, was designed to end a person's life quickly, rather than through prolonged torture. The king and queen of France were eventually executed by guillotine when the Revolution overthrew the monarchy.

Today, like most European countries, France has abolished the death penalty. In fact, among Western industrialized nations, the United States is alone in allowing its citizens to be sentenced to death for certain crimes. For a brief period of time, from 1972 to 1977, there were no executions in the United States as the result of the Supreme Court's decision in *Furman v. Georgia* (1972). This ruling held that the death penalty was unconstitutional because states had no clear-cut standards by which to administer the death penalty: Similar crimes often drew very different sentences, and African Americans were much more likely to be sentenced to death than whites were. The Court based its decision on the Eighth Amendment: "Excessive bail shall not be required, nor excessive fines imposed, nor cruel and unusual punishment inflicted."[2]

However, the court's decision in *Gregg v. Georgia* (1976) upheld revised death penalty statutes that gave jurors specific guidance on when to sentence a convicted criminal to death. Complying with *Gregg*, each state that carries the death penalty has a list of "capital offenses" for which the death penalty may be given. Examples include: murders that were particularly brutal; murders with multiple victims; murders during the commission of another felony, such as a bank robbery; murders of police officers; or murders for hire. Some states include crimes other than murder (such as hijacking) among their list of capital crimes, but it is not clear whether the U.S. Supreme Court or any of the state supreme courts would uphold a death sentence for a crime other than murder.

The first person put to death following *Gregg v. Georgia* was Gary Gilmore of Utah, who was executed by a firing squad in 1977. Several hundred more people have been executed in the United States since then. More than two-thirds of the states allow capital punishment, and a variety of methods are used. These include the firing squad, in which a number of people shoot rifles simultaneously at the condemned person; hanging from the neck with rope; and the gas chamber, which suffocates the condemned person with poisonous gas. For years, the most common method of execution was electrocution using the electric chair, which kills through a series of high-voltage shocks.

Today, most executions in the United States are done by lethal injection of a series of chemicals. First is an anesthetic, which is used—as with surgery—to prevent pain; however, because an unusually high amount of anesthetic is used for a lethal injection, the anesthetic itself can be fatal. Next, a chemical is injected to paralyze the lungs and diaphragm, to make breathing impossible.

In some states, a third chemical injection is used to cause the heart to stop beating.

Many national and international organizations are working to abolish the death penalty in the United States, but a majority of Americans support the death penalty. As a result, capital punishment is often an important issue in local, state, and national elections. The power of capital punishment as a campaign issue is illustrated by the 1988 presidential election. In public opinion polls, Republican Vice President George Bush was trailing Democrat Michael Dukakis, governor of Massachusetts. But the Bush campaign turned around, thanks in large part to the infamous "Willie Horton" television ads.

Willie Horton was a convicted murderer, but under a Massachusetts program while Dukakis was governor, Horton was temporarily released from prison. During his release, he raped and brutally murdered a woman. Bush, who supported the death penalty, used the ads to attack Dukakis, who was opposed to the death penalty and whom Bush characterized as being soft on crime. Although many thought that the commercials showing a mug shot of the African-American convict had racist overtones, the ads were effective in helping Bush win the election.

The Execution of Robert Willie

Although death penalty opponents might be in the minority, many of these abolitionists are very dedicated to the cause. Sister Helen Prejean is one who thinks that capital punishment is wrong, no matter how heinous the crime. A Catholic nun from Louisiana, she became a vocal opponent of the death penalty while serving as a spiritual advisor to death row inmates. At the same time, she also reached out to the victims' families.

If ever a person could test the strength of Prejean's beliefs, it was Robert Willie. His crimes were particularly brutal. In 1978, he murdered a drug dealer by drowning him. In the spring of 1980, he and another man, Joseph Jesse Vaccaro, raped and killed a young woman, Faith Hathaway, stabbing her 17 times and cutting off several of her fingers as she tried to defend herself. Days later, the pair kidnapped a young couple and drove them to Alabama, where the two criminals raped the girl, tied her boyfriend to a tree, and shot him, leaving him paralyzed from the waist down.

Worse yet, Willie's well-publicized actions after his capture suggested that he had no remorse for what he and his partner had done. At the trial for the kidnapping and rape charges for the Alabama crime, Willie blew kisses to the girl he had raped, and made a throat-slashing gesture to the man he had tied to a tree and shot. He also had an image of the grim reaper tattooed across his chest. He told a newspaper reporter, "Hey man, them people's dead. You ain't gonna bring them back by talking about it."[3]

When Prejean first met Willie on Louisiana's death row, she had expected to meet "a wild-eyed, crazed, paranoid type," but was surprised to find him a "polite, soft-spoken, obviously intelligent young man."[4] Nevertheless, she had to come to terms with his horrible crimes while she acted as his spiritual advisor. On numerous occasions, she confronted him with what he had done, and he continued to claim that Vaccaro was responsible for the crimes.

Willie was defiant almost to the end, but his attitude changed somewhat after he was led to the electric chair and addressed Faith Hathaway's mother and stepfather: "I hope you get some relief from my death. Killing people is wrong. That's why you've put me to death. It makes no difference whether it's citizens, countries, or governments. Killing is wrong."[5]

Although she realized that it would be a traumatic experience, Prejean decided to witness the execution:

> When the jolts hit him, the way he was strapped to the chair, his body didn't move much. He lifted somewhat in the chair and his chest pushed against the straps and his hands gripped the edge of the chair, but there wasn't much movement. Three times the current hit, and I couldn't see his face. I had

Sister Helen Prejean believes that capital punishment is wrong, no matter how heinous the crime. A Catholic nun from Louisiana, she became a vocal opponent of the death penalty while serving as a spiritual advisor to death row inmates. She wrote an autobiographical account of her experiences called *Dead Man Walking*, also the title of the film adaptation.

prayed out loud, "God forgive us, forgive all who collaborate in this execution."[6]

Hathaway's parents expressed their satisfaction to the press after the execution. Her stepfather poured himself a celebratory drink and asked a reporter, "Do you want to dance? First thing I'm gonna do is have a drink, then go home and rest."[7]

After the execution, Prejean questioned its purpose. She asked a news reporter, "What have we accomplished by killing Robert Willie? Now two people are dead instead of one, and there will be another funeral and another mother will bury her child."[8] Reverend Jesse Jackson echoed Prejean's sentiments:

[T]he argument that capital punishment eases the grief of a victim's family is questionable, especially in a nation where there are only 25 executions for 25,000 murders each year.... [N]either the death penalty nor its alternatives can substitute for the tremendous loss of a loved one.[9]

When Prejean's book about her experiences, *Dead Man Walking*, was made into a popular movie starring Susan Sarandon and Sean Penn, the news media ran coverage of the death penalty debate, and public interest was aroused. Public awareness of the issue is usually quite high, and each time an execution occurs,

FROM THE BENCH

Gregg v. Georgia, 428 U.S. 153 (1976) (Plurality Opinion)

We address initially the basic contention that the punishment of death for the crime of murder is, under all circumstances, "cruel and unusual" in violation of the Eighth and Fourteenth Amendments of the Constitution....

The Court on a number of occasions has both assumed and asserted the constitutionality of capital punishment. In several cases that assumption provided a necessary foundation for the decision, as the Court was asked to decide whether a particular method of carrying out a capital sentence would be allowed to stand under the Eighth Amendment. But until *Furman v. Georgia*, 408 U.S. 238 (1972), the Court never confronted squarely the fundamental claim that the punishment of death always, regardless of the enormity of the offense or the procedure followed in imposing the sentence, is cruel and unusual punishment in violation of the Constitution. Although this issue was presented and addressed in Furman, it was not resolved by the Court. Four Justices would have held that capital punishment is not unconstitutional per se; two Justices would have reached the opposite conclusion; and three Justices, while agreeing that the statutes then before the Court were invalid as applied, left open the question whether such punishment may ever be imposed. We now hold that the punishment of death does not invariably violate the Constitution.

there is once again an increased interest in capital punishment's pros and cons.

Moral and Religious Issues

There is no clear-cut answer to the question of whether moral or religious values support the death penalty. Some people argue that the Judeo-Christian Bible, which has greatly influenced U.S. laws and morality, supports capital punishment. The Book of Exodus calls for punishment equal to the crime: "life for life, eye for eye, tooth for tooth."[10] But many people question whether these standards are fair today: The same chapter declares that when one man's ox kills another man's servant, then the ox shall be stoned to death and the ox's owner shall pay the servant's master a sum of silver coins.[11]

Today, many church groups, including the Catholic Church, favor abolition of the death penalty. In 1995, Pope John Paul II wrote in his *Evangelium Vitae*:

> [T]he nature and extent of the punishment must be carefully evaluated and decided upon, and ought not go to the extreme of executing the offender except in cases of absolute necessity: in other words, when it would not be possible otherwise to defend society. Today however, as a result of steady improvements in the organization of the penal system, such cases are very rare, if not practically non-existent.[12]

Much of the debate over the death penalty revolves around religious and moral questions that might never be resolved to most people's satisfaction. Still, there are also a number of legal and sociological debates as to whether the United States should retain the death penalty. One of the primary rationales for its continuation is to control crime, but many critics have questioned the death penalty's deterrent effect, and some people even assert that watching the government kill people makes criminals even more likely to commit murder.

Death penalty trials are complicated and always result in lengthy appeals in both the state and federal courts. Many people argue that the system should be streamlined so criminals can be executed more swiftly. However, a great number of people believe that the United States does not provide enough safeguards against mistakes in the system; they point to the cases of innocent people who have been sentenced to death or even executed. In recent years, opponents of the death penalty have pointed to alternatives that they believe would also effectively deter crime, such as the possibility of a sentence of life in prison without parole. Each time an execution draws near, these topics are hotly debated.

Summary

The death penalty is deeply rooted in history, but today the United States is the only Western industrialized nation that continues to use capital punishment. Since the U.S. Supreme Court upheld the practice in *Gregg v. Georgia* (1976), people have been executed by a variety of methods; the most common method of execution today is lethal injection. Although a majority of Americans support the death penalty, it remains controversial. Abolitionists—people who oppose the death penalty—are very dedicated to their cause and very vocal. But the death penalty has many supporters, and is often a key issue in political races.

The Death Penalty Is an Effective Deterrent to Crime

W hen the U.S. Supreme Court ended a nationwide moratorium on executions with the ruling in *Gregg v. Georgia*
(1976), the court cited two major reasons for imposing the death
penalty: retribution and deterrence. Although death penalty
opponents generally argue that retribution is morally unjusti-
fied, they have taken the argument against deterrence a step
further, claiming that deterrence is not supported by the facts.
Supporters of the death penalty reject this argument and believe
that the death penalty *is* an effective deterrent against crime.
In fact, many supporters believe that for each person who is
executed, a number of innocent lives are saved.

The Supreme Court noted in *Gregg* that "there is no convincing empirical evidence either supporting or refuting the
deterrent effect of capital punishment,"[1] thus emphasizing that
the constitutionality of the death penalty does not depend on

its effectiveness as a deterrent. Supporters of capital punishment argue both that the deterrent effect of capital punishment is clear, and that abolitionists miss the point in their attempts to discount the deterrent effect. In the words of political science professor John McAdams:

> If we execute murderers and there is in fact no deterrent effect, we have killed a bunch of murderers. If we fail to execute murderers, and doing so would in fact have deterred other murders, we have allowed the killing of a bunch of innocent victims. I would much rather risk the former. This, to me, is not a tough call.[2]

In fact, some supporters have gone so far as to argue that because the death penalty deters crime, the government is morally obligated to impose capital punishment. In an article in the *Stanford Law Review*, University of Chicago professors Cass Sunstein and Adrian Vermeule review recent statistical studies showing that each execution deters a number of murders. They conclude that if these studies are correct, "A refusal to impose capital punishment will effectively condemn numerous innocent people to death. States that choose life imprisonment, when they might choose capital punishment, are ensuring the deaths of a large number of innocent people."[3] Therefore, they argue, the "death penalty seems morally obligatory if it is the only or most effective means of preventing significant numbers of murders."[4]

Common sense and experience demonstrate capital punishment's deterrent effect.

Some of the strongest arguments for the death penalty's deterrent value are based upon common sense. Put simply, people are afraid of dying, and therefore, the possibility of being sentenced to death for committing certain crimes discourages people from committing those crimes. The experience of the U.S. criminal justice system supports this straightforward logic. Almost everyone who is sentenced to death appeals his or her sentence. Obviously, these people do not wish to die. The inevitability of appeals seems to contradict abolitionists' claims that a sentence of life in prison without parole is as effective a deterrent as a death sentence.

The plea bargaining process also provides evidence that criminals fear the death penalty. A plea bargain is an arrangement between a prosecutor and a criminal defendant (and his or her lawyers), under which the defendant agrees to plead guilty and the prosecutor agrees to recommend a specific sentence. For example, a person who faces up to 10 years in prison for a particular crime might agree to plead guilty in exchange for a sentence of just a couple of years. Prosecutors might offer a plea bargain for various reasons: a fear that the defendant might not be found guilty; an effort to shield a young or traumatized witness from having to testify in court; or a desire to avoid the time and expense of a trial.

The availability of the death penalty makes the plea bargaining process especially effective in murder trials. When someone is charged with killing another person (referred to generally as *homicide*), the prosecutor generally has broad freedoms to charge the defendant with any of a number of crimes, such as first-degree murder or manslaughter. But only certain categories of homicides—so-called *capital murder* offenses—are punishable by the death penalty. By agreeing not to charge the defendant with capital murder, a prosecutor can often persuade the defendant to plead guilty to a lesser charge. The fact that this strategy works shows that criminal defendants fear the death penalty; and this logic can be extended to suggest that because criminals fear the death penalty, the availability of the death penalty deters crime. Legal scholar Charles Keckler writes, "Over the average defendant . . . the influence of the death penalty is apparently quite substantial. In order to achieve a plea of life in prison without the possibility of parole, where the trial outcome is uncertain, it is patent that there must be some penalty that is perceived to be substantially in excess of life imprisonment. . . ."[5]

Capital punishment is needed to curb crime rates.
Although the United States is a world leader in wealth, technology, education, and industry, it nonetheless has much higher

FROM THE BENCH

Gregg v. Georgia, 428 U.S. 153 (1976) (Plurality Opinion)

The death penalty is said to serve two principal social purposes: retribution and deterrence of capital crimes by prospective offenders.

In part, capital punishment is an expression of society's moral outrage at particularly offensive conduct. This function may be unappealing to many, but it is essential in an ordered society that asks its citizens to rely on legal processes rather than self-help to vindicate their wrongs. . . . Indeed, the decision that capital punishment may be the appropriate sanction in extreme cases is an expression of the community's belief that certain crimes are themselves so grievous an affront to humanity that the only adequate response may be the penalty of death.

Statistical attempts to evaluate the worth of the death penalty as a deterrent to crimes by potential offenders have occasioned a great deal of debate. The results simply have been inconclusive. As one opponent of capital punishment has said:

[A]fter all possible inquiry, including the probing of all possible methods of inquiry, we do not know, and for systematic and easily visible reasons cannot know, what the truth about this "deterrent" effect may be. . . .

The inescapable flaw is . . . that social conditions in any state are not constant through time, and that social conditions are not the same in any two states. If an effect were observed (and the observed effects, one way or another, are not large) then one could not at all tell whether any of this effect is attributable to the presence or absence of capital punishment. A "scientific"—that is to say, a soundly based—conclusion crime rates than other Western democracies. Although violent crime rates decreased during the 1990s, the new millennium has seen rates steadily rise. Each year, the Federal Bureau of Investigation (FBI) publishes its Uniform Crime Reporting Program data, collected from law enforcement agencies nationwide. In its latest comprehensive report, for 2005, the FBI noted 16,692 murders during the year—an increase of 3.4 percent from the

is simply impossible, and no methodological path out of this tangle suggests itself."*

Although some of the studies suggest that the death penalty may not function as a significantly greater deterrent than lesser penalties, there is no convincing empirical evidence either supporting or refuting this view. We may nevertheless assume safely that there are murderers, such as those who act in passion, for whom the threat of death has little or no deterrent effect. But for many others, the death penalty undoubtedly is a significant deterrent. There are carefully contemplated murders, such as murder for hire, where the possible penalty of death may well enter into the cold calculus that precedes the decision to act. And there are some categories of murder, such as murder by a life prisoner, where other sanctions may not be adequate.

The value of capital punishment as a deterrent of crime is a complex factual issue, the resolution of which properly rests with the legislatures, which can evaluate the results of statistical studies in terms of their own local conditions and with a flexibility of approach that is not available to the courts.... [Many states' capital punishment] statutes reflect just such a responsible effort to define those crimes and those criminals for which capital punishment is most probably an effective deterrent.

In sum, we cannot say that the judgment of the Georgia Legislature that capital punishment may be necessary in some cases is clearly wrong. Considerations of federalism, as well as respect for the ability of a legislature to evaluate, in terms of its particular State, the moral consensus concerning the death penalty and its social utility as a sanction, require us to conclude, in the absence of more convincing evidence, that the infliction of death as a punishment for murder is not without justification and thus is not unconstitutionally severe.

*C. Black, Capital Punishment: The Inevitability of Caprice and Mistake 25–26 (1974).

Historic rulings on the death penalty

The Supreme Court has answered pivotal questions regarding the constitutionality of the death penalty seven times since 1972.

Supreme Court death penalty rulings, 1972-present

1972	1987	1989	2005
Furman v. Georgia	**McCleskey v. Georgia**	**Stanford v. Kentucky**	**Roper v. Simmons**
Court said death penalty does not violate Constitution, but its application in many states does. Executions essentially end.	Death penalty held as constitutional even when statistics show racial bias was applied.	Ruling upheld constitutionality of executions for juveniles older than 15.	Court ruled that the Constitution forbids the execution of killers under 18 when crime was committed.

1970s   1980s   1990s   2000s

1976	1988	2002
Gregg v. Georgia	**Thompson v. Oklahoma**	**Atkins v. Virginia**
Ruling said state death penalty statute is constitutional. Executions resume.	Justices ruled that offenders younger than 16 may not be executed.	Court said that executing retarded criminals is cruel and unusual punishment.

AP

The sheer volume of U.S. Supreme Court rulings on the death penalty reflects what a controversial issue it continues to be. The graphic above summarizes the most important rulings made since the 1970s.

previous year. Year-by-year comparisons have shown increases almost every year since 2000, even though the report excluded the terrorist acts of September 11, 2001, from the yearly total for that year.

Sociologists blame many factors for the nation's high rate of violent crime. Problems such as drug abuse, gang membership, poverty, and the spread of illegal handguns are not easily solved. Law enforcement officials constantly struggle for increased resources, but even as crime rates continue to escalate, many police forces cannot keep pace. Supporters of the death penalty argue that because it is not feasible to end poverty or drug abuse through social programs, or to remove illegal hand-guns from the streets, the death penalty is needed to help law enforcement keep pace with crime. Supporters say that enforcing the death penalty on a regular basis will result in a statistical decrease in murders.

A landmark 1975 study by economist Isaac Ehrlich[6] attempted to quantify what death penalty supporters had been saying for years—that life lost to execution would save other lives by deterring murders. His study examined murder rates and execution rates nationally during the period from 1933 through 1967. Ehrlich acknowledged that "an apparent negative effect of execution on the murder rate" might be due to the obvious fact that the death penalty prevents people from killing again. However, based on his analysis, he concluded, "punishment in general, and execution in particular exert a unique deterrent effect on potential murderers." His analysis indicated that "an additional execution per year . . . may have resulted, on average, in 7 or 8 fewer murders."

A number of recent studies also conclude that the death penalty deters murders. For example, researchers Hashem Dezhbakhsh, Paul Rubin, and Joanna Shepherd reviewed data from counties nationwide, from 1977 (when the death penalty was reinstated) until 1996. They concluded, "Capital punishment has a strong deterrent effect; each execution results, on average, in eighteen fewer murders—with a margin of error of plus or minus ten."[7]

Naci Mocan and Kaj Gittings examined executions, commutations of death sentences (changing a death sentence to life imprisonment), and other removals of prisoners from death row. They concluded, "The results show that each additional execution decreases homicides by about five, and each additional commutation increases homicides by the same amount, while an additional removal from death row generates one additional murder."[8]

After examining state-level data from 1978 through 1997, economist Paul Zimmerman concluded that each execution has the potential to deter 14 murders.[9] However, in a later study, he found that the method of execution strongly affected its deterrent effect, concluding, "The empirical estimates suggest that the deterrent effect of capital punishment is driven primarily by executions conducted by electrocution."[10]

Criminals avoid committing crimes that carry the death penalty.

States specify "capital offenses" in their death penalty statutes in order to comply with the U.S. Supreme Court's decision in *Furman v. Georgia* (1972). The central holding was that death penalty statutes—as they existed in 1972—violated the Eighth Amendment's ban on "cruel and unusual punishment" because they did not set standards for the types of crimes for which the death penalty was given:

> [W]e deal with a system of law and of justice that leaves to the uncontrolled discretion of judges or juries the determination whether defendants committing these crimes should die or be imprisoned. Under these laws no standards govern the selection of the penalty. People live or die, dependent on the whim of one man or of 12.[11]

As a result of the decision in *Furman*, states rewrote their death penalty statutes, detailing what were capital offenses. A common example is "felony murder," in which a murder is committed during the commission of another felony, such as armed robbery, rape, or kidnapping. Other capital offenses include murdering someone for money, hiring someone to murder another person, and murdering a police officer.

Many death penalty supporters believe that criminals know which crimes are punishable by death, and that criminals avoid these crimes. Anecdotal evidence clearly indicates that the death penalty deters at least *some* crime: Numerous criminals have told law enforcement officers that they specifically avoided committing capital offenses, as opposed to lesser crimes that do not carry the death penalty. For example, one study cataloged incidents from the 1950s through the 1970s in which criminals told law enforcement officials that they "used a fake gun, pretended to be carrying a weapon, or refrained from killing a robbery victim to avoid the death penalty."[12] During the 1970s, the Los Angeles Police Department interviewed nearly a hundred criminals who had not carried weapons while committing crimes, and half of the criminals said fear of the death penalty was a reason for not carrying a weapon.

U.S. Senator Arlen Specter reported that, while he was a prosecutor in Philadelphia, "I saw many cases where professional burglars and robbers refused to carry weapons for fear that a killing would occur and they would be charged with murder in the first degree, carrying the death penalty."[13] The senator gave as a specific example the story of three men who robbed a pharmacist: Two said that they would not participate if the third carried a gun. Although the third man pretended to put the gun away, he secretly brought it with him and ended up killing the pharmacist. The first two were spared the death penalty because they did not know that the third man had the gun.

Capital punishment is needed to ensure that murderers will not kill again.

Supporters of the death penalty reject an argument frequently made by abolitionists—that the sentence of life in prison without possibility of parole is as effective as the death penalty in deterring murders. In particular, say supporters, the death penalty is needed to stop convicted murderers from killing again. A sentence of life in prison without parole cannot achieve this objective.

The main flaw in substituting a sentence of life in prison without parole for the death penalty is that such a sentence does not carry the finality of the death penalty. Although a person might be sentenced to life in prison without parole, there is no guarantee that the person will remain in prison forever. One possibility is that the state legislature might change laws to allow people under such a sentence to qualify for parole (for example, through good behavior). Another possibility is that a person could use his or her time in prison to bring endless legal challenges to his or her conviction. This could perhaps ultimately overturn the sentence on a technicality of law, such as a mistake in the search warrant.

Of course, there is also the very real possibility that a person who is part of the general prison population and not kept on the more secure "death row" could eventually escape from prison. By allowing the convicted criminal the possibility of one day regaining his or her freedom through legal or illegal means, the sentence of life in prison without parole does not deter crime as effectively as the death penalty. Death penalty supporters also argue that a person sentenced to life in prison without parole—in the absence of a death penalty—could kill another prisoner or a prison guard.[14] From a practical standpoint, the inmate already facing the maximum penalty allowed by law has no legal disincentive to kill again. With nothing to risk, and the only means to freedom being escape, logic says that a prisoner facing life in prison without parole would be likely to kill in order to escape.

Summary

Many people believe that the death penalty deters crime and is therefore needed to curb soaring crime rates. Some arguments for deterrence are based upon common sense: Criminals, once caught, make efforts to avoid the death penalty; criminals tell police that they avoid crimes punishable by death; and murderers who are executed obviously cannot murder again. Supporters of the death penalty frequently cite research indicating that each execution has the potential to prevent more murders.

The Death Penalty Is Not an Effective Deterrent to Crime

The theory that the death penalty deters crime is supported by anecdotes, such as those of criminals who refused to carry weapons because they feared the death penalty. It is also supported by some studies, such as those conducted by Isaac Ehrlich, which assert that each execution deters eight homicides. Nevertheless, many opponents of the death penalty steadfastly maintain that it does *not* deter crime. In fact, many abolitionists believe that the death penalty actually *encourages* crime.

They cite studies indicating that murder rates increase after executions, thus supporting the "brutalization theory." This theory holds that when a state or the federal government executes a prisoner, the very violence of the act devalues human life in the eyes of society and makes individual members of society more likely to kill.

Statistics show that the death penalty does not deter crime.

Arguments against the deterrent effect of capital punishment have their roots in landmark studies that were conducted before Ehrlich's study. Studies conducted by criminologist Thorsten Sellin, beginning in the 1950s, remain particularly important. Sellin made two major types of comparisons. First, he compared the homicide rates in sets of neighboring states, some of which allowed capital punishment and some of which did not. He compared the following states: Indiana and Ohio, which had a death penalty statute, to Michigan, which did not; Iowa (death penalty) to Minnesota and Wisconsin (no death penalty); South Dakota and Nebraska (death penalty) to North Dakota (no death penalty); New Hampshire and Vermont (death penalty) to Maine (no death penalty); and Massachusetts and Connecticut (death penalty) to Rhode Island (no death penalty). States without the death penalty had similar or lower homicide rates in comparison to death penalty states.

Then, in 1967, Sellin published a study examining changes in homicide rates in states that had either adopted a capital punishment statute or had eliminated the death penalty: Arizona, Colorado, Delaware, Iowa, Kansas, Maine, Missouri, Oregon, South Dakota, Tennessee, and Washington. The study found that neither instituting nor discontinuing the death penalty had any significant effect on the rate of homicides.

In the years following Isaac Ehrlich's studies, a number of economists and social scientists attempted to support or disprove Ehrlich's assertion that each execution prevented eight murders. In his dissenting opinion to *Gregg v. Georgia* (1976), Justice Thurgood Marshall summed up the major criticisms of Ehrlich's conclusion that each execution prevented an average of eight homicides.

Marshall first pointed out that Ehrlich's study looked at the nation as a whole, rather than examining statistics on a state-by-state basis:

It has been suggested, for example, that the study is defective because it compares execution and homicide rates on a nationwide, rather than a state-by-state, basis. The aggregation of data from all States—including those that have abolished the death penalty—obscures the relationship between murder and execution rates. Under Ehrlich's methodology, a decrease in the execution risk in one State combined with an increase in the murder rate in another State would, all other things being equal, suggest a deterrent effect that quite obviously would not exist. Indeed, a deterrent effect would be suggested if, once again all other things being equal, one State abolished the death penalty and experienced no change in the murder rate, while another State experienced an increase in the murder rate.[1]

In other words, Ehrlich failed to examine whether nationwide decreases in homicide rates were due to lower homicide rates in states that had the death penalty or in states that did not have the death penalty.

Additionally, Marshall criticized Ehrlich's analysis because the results were not consistent during the entire time period of the study, 1933 to 1969:

The most compelling criticism of the Ehrlich study is that its conclusions are extremely sensitive to the choice of the time period included in the regression analysis. Analysis of Ehrlich's data reveals that all empirical support for the deterrent effect of capital punishment disappears when the five most recent years are removed from his time series—that is to say, whether a decrease in the execution risk corresponds to an increase or a decrease in the murder rate depends on the ending point of the sample period. This finding has cast severe doubts on the reliability of Ehrlich's tentative conclusions. Indeed, a recent regression study, based on Ehrlich's theoretical model but using cross-section state data for the years 1950 and 1960, found no support for the conclusion that executions act as a deterrent.[2]

Essentially, Marshall accused Ehrlich of manipulating the data: Ehrlich's conclusions might have been valid for the years he selected for his study. However, had Ehrlich chosen different years for the study, he would not have been able to establish that the death penalty lowers homicide rates. Thus, Marshall concluded, "The Ehrlich study, in short, is of little, if any, assistance in assessing the deterrent impact of the death penalty."[3]

In recent years, abolitionists have continued to assail the conclusions of studies finding a deterrent effect. Testifying before the Massachusetts legislature in 2005, Columbia University professor Jeffrey Fagan argued:

> Recent studies claiming that executions reduce murders have fueled the revival of deterrence as a rationale to expand the use of capital punishment. Such strong claims are not unusual in either the social or natural sciences, but like nearly all claims of strong causal effects from any social or legal intervention, the claims of a "new deterrence" fall apart under close scrutiny. These new studies are fraught with technical and conceptual errors: inappropriate methods of statistical analysis, failures to consider all the relevant factors that drive murder rates, missing data on key variables in key states, the tyranny of a few outlier states and years, weak to non-existent tests of concurrent effects of incarceration, statistical confounding of murder rates with death sentences, failure to consider the general performance of the criminal justice system, and the absence of any direct test of deterrence.[4]

Fagan's biggest criticism was that studies of deterrence attempt to simplify extremely complex societal influences without clearly identifying all of the factors that might influence murder rates. Additionally, he points out that most of the deterrent effect found nationally can be attributed to states such as Texas, which he

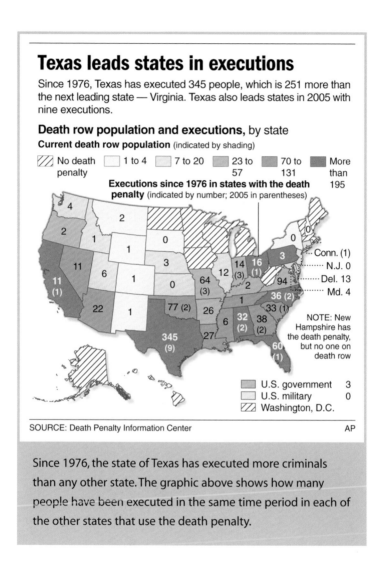

Texas leads states in executions

Since 1976, Texas has executed 345 people, which is 251 more than the next leading state — Virginia. Texas also leads states in 2005 with nine executions.

Death row population and executions, by state

Current death row population (indicated by shading)

| ▨ No death penalty | ☐ 1 to 4 | ☐ 7 to 20 | ■ 23 to 57 | ■ 70 to 131 | ■ More than 195 |

Executions since 1976 in states with the death penalty (indicated by number; 2005 in parentheses)

Conn. (1)
N.J. 0
Del. 13
Md. 4

NOTE: New Hampshire has the death penalty, but no one on death row

■ U.S. government   3
☐ U.S. military   0
▨ Washington, D.C.

SOURCE: Death Penalty Information Center   AP

Since 1976, the state of Texas has executed more criminals than any other state. The graphic above shows how many people have been executed in the same time period in each of the other states that use the death penalty.

classifies as "outlier states" because they depart from the national trend and execute significantly higher numbers of convicts.

Murderers do not think about the consequences of their actions.

In addition to discounting statistical evidence supporting the death penalty, abolitionists offer philosophical and psycho-logical explanations as to why the death penalty does not deter crime. In his book condemning the death penalty, Rev. Jesse Jackson offers the following theory:

> Deterrence depends on would-be murderers identifying with the executed killer. The problem with that logic is that countless psychological studies show that we identify with those whom we admire or envy. Condemned prisoners who arrive at the electric chair are a wretched lot. Since they are generally loners who are uneducated and have committed brutal and cowardly crimes, it is highly unlikely that calculating killers would identify with them. The contrast they see between themselves and the condemned may actually lead prospective killers to determine that the death penalty is reserved only for people unlike themselves.[5]

Abolitionists suggest that the very nature of most capital crimes makes them difficult to deter. For example, many murders are committed in the heat of passion, and the murderer is not thinking of the consequences of his or her actions. Consider this first-hand account:

> [My wife] came out and said, "Look, please do me this favor and give me a divorce." At that moment I felt cold hatred for her inside me.... My hate for her exploded then, and I ... started pounding her in the face with my fist. She put her arms up and covered her face, so I ran and got my rifle.... I got so mad and felt so much hate for her that I just started shooting her again and again.[6]

Abolitionists argue that even murderers "who cold-bloodedly plan and carry out their crimes ... think they are too clever to be caught. The death penalty cannot be a deterrent to them because they are convinced they will escape punishment of any kind."[7] One of the most famous murder cases of the twentieth century illustrates this principle.

Nathan Leopold Jr. and Richard Loeb were extremely intelligent young men who came from wealthy families and who shared a morbid desire to commit the perfect crime. After months of planning, on May 21, 1924, the pair kidnapped a teenage boy who lived in their affluent Chicago neighborhood. They then killed him and hid his body in a park in a remote part of the city. They went on with their social and academic activities as usual while trying to collect a ransom from the boy's father, to whom they lied and said that the boy was still alive. They never once imagined that they would be caught, and they probably would not have been, had Leopold not accidentally left a rare, expensive pair of eyeglasses at the crime scene. Killers who do not believe that they will be caught almost certainly do not consider possible punishments.

Other murderers might be so out of touch with reality that they do not consider the consequences of their crimes. Gary Cone, a Vietnam veteran who was sentenced to death for a double homicide, explained that his experiences in Vietnam had caused him great distress that led to drug abuse and developing post-traumatic stress disorder (PTSD): "My visions in sleep were clouded by the sight of a buddy's head being blown off, and dying women and children I had seen left in the fields. The Vietcong would often torture and cut the children in half."[8]

After returning from Vietnam, Cone—like many Vietnam veterans—met with rejection everywhere, especially when he looked for a job. Although he did not have a criminal history, he turned to a life of crime. Despite serving a short prison term, his criminal life continued to spiral out of control. According to court records:

> [Cone] robbed a Memphis jewelry store of approximately $112,000 in merchandise on a Saturday in August 1980. Shortly after the 12:45 p.m. robbery, a police officer in an unmarked vehicle spotted respondent driving at a normal

speed and began to follow him. After a few blocks, respondent accelerated, prompting a high-speed chase through midtown Memphis and into a residential neighborhood where respondent abandoned his vehicle. Attempting to flee, respondent shot an officer who tried to apprehend him, shot a citizen who confronted him, and, at gunpoint, demanded that another hand over his car keys. As a police helicopter hovered overhead, respondent tried to shoot the fleeing car owner, but was frustrated because his gun was out of ammunition.

Throughout the afternoon and into the next morning, respondent managed to elude detection as police combed the surrounding area. In the meantime, officers inventorying his car found an array of illegal and prescription drugs, the stolen merchandise, and more than $2,400 in cash. Respondent reappeared early Sunday morning when he drew a gun on an elderly resident who refused to let him in to use her telephone. Later that afternoon, respondent broke into the home of Shipley and Cleopatra Todd, aged 93 and 79 years old, and killed them by repeatedly beating them about the head with a blunt instrument. He moved their bodies so that they would not be visible from the front and rear doors and ransacked the first floor of their home. After shaving his beard, respondent traveled to Florida. He was arrested there for robbing a drugstore in Pompano Beach. He admitted killing the Todds and shooting the police officer.[9]

Cone claims the shoot-out with the police caused him to have a flashback: "[T]he shooting . . . and the tear gas brought my mind swiftly back to the jungles of Vietnam. . . . I actually thought I was back in the war." Regarding the Todds, he said: "[T]wo people were dead. I don't remember killing them, but I know I must have. I remember thinking I was in the jungle of Vietnam, with the Cong chasing me, trying to kill me before I was arrested."[10]

The Supreme Court did acknowledge that many murderers are not deterred by the threat of the death penalty when it held in *Atkins v. Virginia* (2002) that the Eighth Amendment's ban on cruel and unusual punishment prevented states from executing mentally retarded people. The Court ruled that mentally retarded people's "diminished ability to understand and process information . . . make[s] it less likely that they can process the information of the possibility of execution as a penalty and, as a result, control their conduct based upon that information."[11]

The death penalty might actually increase crime rates.

Perhaps the strongest argument against the deterrent effect of capital punishment can be found in a number of studies that indicate that the homicide rate actually increases after an execution. Studies conducted in London, Philadelphia, Oklahoma, and California show a significant increase in homicides in those areas shortly after an execution took place. In 1980, William Bowers and Glenn Pierce examined homicide rates during the period from 1907 to 1963 in New York, which at the time was the state that executed the most people. Homicide rates generally rose in a month that followed an execution. Bowers and Pierce explained this surprising result through the "brutalization theory." This is the idea that when the state takes a person's life by execution, it devalues human life in the eyes of its citizens, making them more likely to commit murder.

In fact, in states where executions are infrequent, the brutalization theory seems to be supported by facts. Excluding six states (South Carolina, Florida, Texas, Georgia, Delaware, and Nevada) that collectively have executed many people, Joanna Shepherd noted that other death penalty states actually show a spike in murders after an execution. "The many states with [low] numbers of executions . . . may be executing people needlessly. Indeed, instead of deterring crime, the executions may be inducing additional murders: a rough total estimate is that, in the many states where executions induce murders rather than deter them, executions cause an additional 250 murders per year," Shepherd concluded.[12]

Michael Kronenwetter offers alternative theories as to why the threat of the death penalty might actually encourage murder:

FROM THE BENCH

Atkins v. Virginia, 536 U.S. 304 (2002)

Given the well-known fact that anticrime legislation is far more popular than legislation providing protections for persons guilty of violent crime, the large number of States prohibiting the execution of mentally retarded persons (and the complete absence of States passing legislation reinstating the power to conduct such executions) provides powerful evidence that today our society views mentally retarded offenders as categorically less culpable than the average criminal. The evidence carries even greater force when it is noted that the legislatures that have addressed the issue have voted overwhelmingly in favor of the prohibition.

This consensus unquestionably reflects widespread judgment about the relative culpability of mentally retarded offenders, and the relationship between mental retardation and the penological purposes served by the death penalty. Additionally, it suggests that some characteristics of mental retardation undermine the strength of the procedural protections that our capital jurisprudence steadfastly guards.

As discussed above, clinical definitions of mental retardation require not only subaverage intellectual functioning, but also significant limitations in adaptive skills such as communication, self-care, and self-direction that became manifest before age 18. Mentally retarded persons frequently know the difference between right and wrong and are competent to stand trial. Because of their impairments, however, by definition they have diminished capacities to understand and process information, to communicate, to abstract from mistakes and learn from experience, to engage in logical reasoning, to control impulses, and to understand the reactions of others. There is no evidence that they are more likely to engage in criminal conduct than others, but there is abundant evidence that they often act on impulse rather than pursuant to a premeditated plan, and that in group settings they are followers rather than leaders. Their deficiencies do not warrant an exemption from criminal sanctions, but they do diminish their personal culpability....

The threat of capital punishment raises the stakes of getting caught. Anyone already subject to the death penalty has little to lose by killing again and again. Their potential sentence cannot be made any worse than it already is. This means

With respect to deterrence—the interest in preventing capital crimes by prospective offenders—"it seems likely that 'capital punishment can serve as a deterrent only when murder is the result of premeditation and deliberation,'"... Exempting the mentally retarded from that punishment will not affect the "cold calculus that precedes the decision" of other potential murderers.... Indeed, that sort of calculus is at the opposite end of the spectrum from behavior of mentally retarded offenders. The theory of deterrence in capital sentencing is predicated upon the notion that the increased severity of the punishment will inhibit criminal actors from carrying out murderous conduct. Yet it is the same cognitive and behavioral impairments that make these defendants less morally culpable—for example, the diminished ability to understand and process information, to learn from experience, to engage in logical reasoning, or to control impulses—that also make it less likely that they can process the information of the possibility of execution as a penalty and, as a result, control their conduct based upon that information. Nor will exempting the mentally retarded from execution lessen the deterrent effect of the death penalty with respect to offenders who are not mentally retarded. Such individuals are unprotected by the exemption and will continue to face the threat of execution. Thus, executing the mentally retarded will not measurably further the goal of deterrence....

Our independent evaluation of the issue reveals no reason to disagree with the judgment of "the legislatures that have recently addressed the matter" and concluded that death is not a suitable punishment for a mentally retarded criminal. We are not persuaded that the execution of mentally retarded criminals will measurably advance the deterrent or the retributive purpose of the death penalty. Construing and applying the Eighth Amendment in the light of our "evolving standards of decency," we therefore conclude that such punishment is excessive and that the Constitution "places a substantive restriction on the State's power to take the life" of a mentally retarded offender....

that criminals who already face death for previous crimes are more likely to kill to avoid capture.[13]

Additionally, once captured, a prisoner facing the death penalty has nothing to lose by killing guards or fellow prisoners.

Anecdotal evidence suggests that some people actually look at the death penalty as a means of committing suicide. For example, before his 1992 execution, Lloyd Wayne Hampton gave the following reason for having murdered a 69-year-old man:

> I had given up trying to make it. What was I going to do? . . . I either had to put myself in a position of being killed by someone else or committing suicide. At that point, I had strong beliefs about not killing myself. . . . So I put myself in a position to have the state kill me.[14]

Summary

Abolitionists dispute the deterrent effect of the death penalty, accusing supporters of manipulating statistics. In some of the most important earlier studies, it was shown that when similar states are compared, crime rates are not lower in states with the death penalty. Abolitionists also criticize a new wave of deterrence studies, saying that they do not carefully consider other factors that affect murder rates, and that a few states account for most or all of the deterrent effect. Abolitionists attribute the lack of deterrence to the reality that criminals either do not think about the consequences of their actions or believe that they will never be caught.

Reducing Limits on Capital Punishment Would Make It More Effective

In addition to pointing to the deterrent effect, death penalty supporters further argue that capital punishment would be much more effective if convicted criminals were executed more swiftly. Responding to criticisms of deterrence data, professors Cass Sunstein and Adrian Vermeule of the University of Chicago noted, "Even if [it was] true [that current evidence of deterrence is weak], we could certainly imagine a regime of capital punishment that would, in fact, deter homicides."[1] When a convicted criminal is sentenced to death, it is not only the end of a lengthy trial requiring great effort on the parts of the prosecutors and the court system; it is also the beginning, in most cases, of a lengthy process of appealing the sentence to higher courts, perhaps all the way to the U.S. Supreme Court. The appeals process can take many years, and in many states, appeals courts are required to hear appeals of all death sentences, regardless of the merits of the case. Death penalty supporters want to remove these obstacles and execute people more swiftly.

Capital trials are too lengthy and impose too many costs on the court system.

A capital trial is much different from other criminal trials, even other murder trials. Because of procedural safeguards imposed by the U.S. Supreme Court, state courts, and state statutes, a capital trial lasts longer and requires more money than other criminal trials. Although people commonly attribute the cost of capital punishment to the post-trial appeals process, recent studies confirm that "the bulk of death penalty costs occur at the *trial* level."[2] As a result, many smaller counties are experiencing financial crises caused by death penalty trials, and more and more district attorneys are hesitating to seek the death penalty.

Many of the costs are procedural. For example, in capital cases, two public defenders are assigned to defendants who cannot afford to hire their own lawyers. In other criminal cases, however, the defendant is only entitled to one court-appointed lawyer. Other costs are due to special efforts taken to ensure that the jury has as much information as possible upon which to base its determination of guilt or innocence and its decision about whether or not to impose the death penalty. Investigators and expert witnesses—who testify about crime scene evidence or the defendant's intelligence or sanity, for example—are common in capital cases, and the cost of hiring them is typically borne by the court system. Also, capital trials include a separate sentencing phase in front of a jury, which must make the decision whether or not to impose the death penalty. In other criminal trials, a judge determines the sentence.

As might be expected, defense lawyers in capital cases typically take extra efforts to prevent their clients from being sentenced to death. As trials grow longer, they impose more costs on the court system. The jury selection process in capital trials is a painstaking process in which potential jurors are asked about their opinions on capital punishment. Generally, many more potential jurors are rejected than in other jury selection processes. Additionally, defense lawyers typically make many motions to exclude evidence, each of which must be ruled upon by the judge.

The result of the special procedures used in capital trials is that imposing the death penalty on a defendant can be extremely expensive. Abolitionist Richard Dieter noted: "In Texas, a death penalty case costs taxpayers an average of $2.3 million, about three times the cost of imprisoning someone in a single cell at the highest security level for 40 years. In Florida, each execution is costing the state $3.2 million."[3]

Although Dieter and other critics cite high costs as a reason to abolish the death penalty, supporters of the death penalty believe that the solution is to streamline the legal process by eliminating some of the procedural safeguards. But pro–death penalty federal judge Alex Kozinski believes that because overturning U.S. Supreme Court jurisprudence would be impractical, if not impossible, a more practical approach is needed: "[S]tate legislatures should draft narrow statutes that reserve the death penalty for only the most heinous criminals . . . mass murderers, hired killers, airplane bombers, for example."[4] Although such a solution would involve a compromise by death penalty supporters, Kozinski believes that it would allow "the people, through their elected representatives [to] reassert meaningful control over the process," rather than allowing the courts to decide "on an ad hoc, irrational basis" who lives and who dies. To many death penalty supporters, however, it is the courts, and not the public, that should be willing to compromise.

Juries are denied valuable information in the sentencing hearing.

In order to protect the rights of criminal defendants, criminal procedure places limits on the information that a jury is allowed to hear. Although victims' rights advocates won a major victory in *Payne v. Tennessee*, some say that additional reforms are needed. An example of a protection that some death penalty supporters believe is excessive is the rule established by *Dawson v. Delaware*, 503 U.S. 159 (1992). In that case, the U.S. Supreme Court overturned the death sentence of David Dawson, who had been convicted of brutally murdering a woman and stealing her car after he had escaped from prison. Although the trial judge did not allow the prosecutors to introduce evidence that Dawson had Nazi symbols tattooed all over his body, the judge did allow the prosecutor to introduce evidence that Dawson belonged to the Aryan Brotherhood, "a white racist prison gang." The court held that exposing this evidence violated Dawson's First Amendment right "to join groups and associate with others holding similar beliefs," reasoning:

> Even if the Delaware group to which Dawson allegedly belongs is racist, those beliefs, so far as we can determine, had no relevance to the sentencing proceeding in this case. For example, the Aryan Brotherhood evidence was not tied in any way to the murder of Dawson's victim.[5]

In a dissent, Justice Clarence Thomas warned that the Court's decision resulted in a "double standard" that prevented the jury from developing a true sense of the defendant's character:

> To prove his good character ... Dawson introduced evidence that he had acted kindly toward his family, and that he had earned good time credits while in prison.... Dawson also introduced evidence of his membership and participation in various respectable organizations, including the Green Tree Program (described only as a "drug and alcohol program"), Alcoholics Anonymous ... and certain therapy and counseling groups....

The Court's opinion suggests that the Constitution now imposes a double standard for determining relevance: a standard easy for defendants to satisfy, but difficult for prosecutors. [A] capital defendant has a right to introduce all relevant mitigating evidence. Capital defendants, as a result, regularly introduce character evidence that allows juries to consider their abstract beliefs and associational rights . . . for example, membership in a church . . . religious rebirth . . . conversion to Christianity . . . [and] former membership in the Cub Scouts[.] I see no way to hold that this evidence has relevance, but that Dawson's gang membership does not.

A double standard for determining relevance may distort the picture presented to the jury. In this case, Dawson himself chose to introduce evidence of certain good character traits. Unless the State had responded with evidence of other, bad traits, the jury could not possibly have made a fair and balanced determination. Membership in Alcoholics Anonymous might suggest a good character, but membership in the Aryan Brotherhood just as surely suggests a bad one. The jury could not have assessed Dawson's overall character without both.[6]

The capital punishment appeals process is too lengthy and costly.

The appeals process for a criminal sentenced to death can last decades, in part because a condemned criminal can appeal his or her conviction to the state's appeals courts and supreme court, each of which might overturn the decision, order the lower court to reexamine an issue, or call for a whole new trial. Additionally, someone convicted in state court may appeal his or her conviction or death sentence to federal district courts, appeals courts, and the U.S. Supreme Court through a process known as *habeas corpus*. A writ, or order, of habeas corpus is an order to have a prisoner appear in front of a judge on a certain day at a certain time.

Supporters of the death penalty say that this lengthy process undermines the deterrent effect of capital punishment. It is argued that criminals do not fear the death penalty as much because even those sentenced to death often survive for decades on death row or eventually have their sentences overturned. In a 2003 study of state-level data, Joanna Shepherd concludes, "longer waits on death row before execution lessen the deterrence. Specifically, one less murder is committed for every 2.75-year reduction in death row waits."[7]

In a later article, Shepherd further discussed the impact of legal delays upon the deterrent effect of capital punishment. Noting that economists uniformly had concluded that the death penalty *does* deter murder, while sociologists and law professors generally had concluded that it *does not* deter murder, she argued that this conflict could be explained by the ineffectiveness of the way the death penalty is administered. To explain the seeming inconsistency, she argued that the brutalization theory might be correct—that an isolated execution or two might increase murders, but that a consistently applied death penalty would have enough of a deterrent effect to overcome the brutalization effect and deter additional murders. Specifically, she concluded:

> In states with fewer than a threshold of approximately nine executions during the sample period, each execution increases the number of murders. In states that exceed the threshold, executions deter murder. Deterrence and nondeterrence states are not different in [factors] such as how much publicity executions receive, the characteristics of the executed people, and the method of execution.[8]

Death penalty supporters won major victories with the passage of the Antiterrorism and Effective Death Penalty Act of 1996, which limits the use of the habeas corpus process by condemned criminals. Also supportive of the death penalty was the USA Patriot Improvement and Reauthorization Act of 2005, which imposes time limits on habeas corpus proceedings. "Recent legislation to shorten the wait should strengthen capital punishment's deterrent effect," Shepherd predicted.[9]

Despite these reforms, the appeals process can still go on, seemingly forever. Gary Cone, the Vietnam veteran who was convicted in 1982 of killing an elderly couple two years earlier, was still having appeals heard by the federal courts in 2007—25 years after his death sentence was handed down. In 2002, the U.S. Supreme Court ruled on an issue that Cone initially had raised in 1984: that his trial lawyer failed to provide him with effective representation because the lawyer passed up the opportunity to offer a closing argument. Although a number of state and federal courts accepted the lawyer's explanation that it had been a strategic decision based upon the tone of the proceedings, a federal appeals court overruled the previous decisions. The state appealed the decision, and the U.S. Supreme Court reversed the lower court, upholding Cone's conviction and death sentence in *Bell v. Cone* (2002).

The Court did not decide whether or not Cone's lawyer had provided him with ineffective representation. Rather, the Tennessee Court of Appeals had already decided this issue, and so the Supreme Court did not have to decide the issue based on the facts. Because the Antiterrorism and Effective Death Penalty Act of 1996 limits federal habeas corpus proceedings, the Supreme Court's only inquiry was whether "the Tennessee Court of Appeals applied [the law] to the facts of his case in an objectively unreasonable manner."[10]

But even the Supreme Court's 2002 decision did not put an end to the legal saga. In 2004, the U.S. Court of Appeals for the Sixth Circuit granted Cone another order of habeas corpus based on its conclusion that the Tennessee law imposing the death penalty for "especially heinous, atrocious, or cruel" crimes, which

THE LETTER OF THE LAW

Excerpt from Antiterrorism and Effective Death Penalty Act of 1996 ("Aedpa") 28 U.S.C.

Sec. 2254. State custody; remedies in Federal courts

(a) The Supreme Court ... shall entertain an application for a writ of habeas corpus in behalf of a person in custody pursuant to the judgment of a State court only on the ground that he is in custody in violation of the Constitution or laws or treaties of the United States.

(b)(1) An application for a writ of habeas corpus on behalf of a person in custody pursuant to the judgment of a State court [generally] shall not be granted unless it appears that ... the applicant has exhausted the remedies available in the courts of the State[.]

   (2) An application for a writ of habeas corpus may be denied on the merits, notwithstanding the failure of the applicant to exhaust the remedies available in the courts of the State....

(d) An application for a writ of habeas corpus on behalf of a person in custody pursuant to the judgment of a State court [generally] shall not be granted with respect to any claim that was adjudicated on the merits in State court proceedings....

(e)(1) In a proceeding instituted by an application for a writ of habeas corpus by a person in custody pursuant to the judgment of a State court, a determination of a factual issue made by a State court shall be presumed to be correct. The applicant shall have the burden of rebutting the presumption of correctness by clear and convincing evidence....

   (i) The ineffectiveness or incompetence of counsel during Federal or State collateral post-conviction proceedings shall not be a ground for relief....

Sec. 2263. Filing of habeas corpus application; time requirements; tolling rules

(a) Any application ... for habeas corpus relief ... must be filed in the appropriate district court not later than 180 days after final State court affirmance of the conviction ... [but this time may be extended by] an additional period not to exceed 30 days, if ... a showing of good cause is made....

Sec. 2264. Scope of Federal review; district court adjudications

(a) Whenever a State prisoner under capital sentence files a petition for habeas corpus relief to which this chapter applies, the district court shall only consider a claim or claims that have been raised and decided on the merits in the State courts, unless the failure to raise the claim properly is—

(1) the result of State action in violation of the Constitution or laws of the United States;

(2) the result of the Supreme Court's recognition of a new Federal right that is made retroactively applicable; or

(3) based on a factual predicate that could not have been discovered through the exercise of due diligence in time to present the claim for State or Federal post-conviction review. . . .

Sec. 2266. Limitation periods for determining applications and motions

(a) The adjudication of any application . . . by a person under sentence of death, shall be given priority by the district court and by the court of appeals over all noncapital matters.

(b)(1)(A) A district court shall render a final determination and enter a final judgment on any application for a writ of habeas corpus brought under this chapter in a capital case not later than 180 days after the date on which the application is filed.

(B) A district court shall afford the parties at least 120 days in which to complete all actions, including the preparation of all pleadings and briefs, and if necessary, a hearing, prior to the submission of the case for decision.

(C)(i) A district court may delay for not more than one additional 30-day period beyond the period specified in subparagraph (A), the rendering of a determination of an application for a writ of habeas corpus if the court issues a written order making a finding, and stating the reasons for the finding, that the ends of justice that would be served by allowing the delay outweigh the best interests of the public and the applicant in a speedy disposition of the application. . . .

(iii) No delay in disposition shall be permissible because of general congestion of the court's calendar. . . .

(3) The time limitations under this section shall not be construed to entitle an applicant to a stay of execution, to which the applicant would otherwise not be entitled, for the purpose of litigating any application or appeal.

(4)(A) The failure of a court to meet or comply with a time limitation under this section shall not be a ground for granting relief from a judgment of conviction or sentence.

the state's Supreme Court had applied in 1984, was unconstitutionally vague.[11] In 2005 the U.S. Supreme Court reversed the appeals court, noting:

> [The federal habeas corpus law] demands that state-court decisions be given the benefit of the doubt. . . . Even absent such a presumption in the state court's favor, however, we would still conclude in this case that the state court applied the narrower construction of the "heinous, atrocious, or cruel" aggravating circumstance. The State Supreme Court's reasoning in this case closely tracked its rationale for affirming the death sentences in other cases in which it expressly applied a narrowed construction of the same "heinous, atrocious, or cruel" aggravator. . . . The facts the court relied on to affirm the jury's verdict—that the elderly victims attempted to resist, that their deaths were not instantaneous, that respondent's actions towards them were "unspeakably brutal" and that they endured "terror, fright, and horror" before being killed . . . match, almost exactly, the reasons the state court gave when it held the evidence in [a 1982 case] to be sufficient to satisfy the torture prong of the narrowed "heinous, atrocious, or cruel" aggravating circumstance.[12]

After the Supreme Court's decision, the Court of Appeals heard a third appeal for habeas corpus brought by Cone, which it rejected in June 2007, in part because of the Supreme Court's ruling and in part because of its rejection of additional claims by Cone.[13]

Twice, the Supreme Court put an end to an appeal by Cone by applying federal laws limiting appeals by death row inmates. Although the Supreme Court's 2005 decision and the lower court's 2007 decision seemingly promised to put an end to the ordeal of the families of Cone's victims, Cone was still on death row 27 years after his crime. Many death penalty supporters argue that further reforms are needed, because 27 years is too long for victims' families to wait for closure.

Summary

Many argue that it is too difficult to execute criminals for their crimes. Capital trials are long and expensive and offer too many protections to accused criminals. The appeals process can last for decades. Although recent federal laws should curb the appeals process somewhat, many people would like to see further reforms.

It Is Too Easy to Convict and Execute People

Despite claims from death penalty supporters, victims' rights groups, and prosecutors that enforcing the death penalty is too difficult and costly, many abolitionists steadfastly believe that the opposite is true: that it is too easy to convict someone and sentence him or her to death. In addition to criticizing specific elements of the capital trial and sentencing procedures, abolitionists also point to examples of cases in which people have been wrongfully sentenced to death or even executed.

Victims' families have too great a role in capital punishment.

Since the early 1980s, in response to court decisions expanding the rights of the accused, crime victims and their families and the families of murder victims began to organize the victims' rights movement. Many states have passed victims' rights laws, which, among other things, require victims and their families to be notified of criminal proceedings, entitle them to monetary compensation, and guarantee their right to testify at trials and sentencing hearings.

Until 1991, crime victims' families did not have the right to offer testimony at sentencing hearings in capital trials. The Supreme Court had held, in cases such as *Booth v. Maryland* (1987), that "victim impact statements," which describe how a crime has affected murder victims' families, were not admissible. John Booth had murdered an elderly Baltimore couple, and according to the victim impact statement prepared by the Division of Parole and Probation:

> The son, for example, said that he suffers from lack of sleep and depression, and is "fearful for the first time in his life." . . . He said that in his opinion, his parents were "butchered like animals." . . . The daughter said she also suffers from lack of sleep, and that since the murders she has become withdrawn and distrustful. She stated that she can no longer watch violent movies or look at kitchen knives without being reminded of the murders.[1]

The court overturned Booth's sentence, reasoning that although "[o]ne can understand the grief and anger of the family," the victim impact statement would "inflame the jury" and prevent it from basing its sentence on "relevant evidence."[2]

Four years later, the Court reversed itself, holding in *Payne v. Tennessee* (1991) that victim impact statements are admissible. While even steadfast abolitionists such as Sister Helen Prejean acknowledge the validity of the anger of crime victims and their families—she has been active in victim support groups—abolitionists do not believe that this anger serves as a justification for capital punishment. Abolitionists believe that the Supreme Court went too far in *Payne*. As Justice Stevens noted in his dissent, the decision tipped the balance against the defendant and greatly increased the probability of execution, based on factors other than the defendant's guilt:

> Today's majority has obviously been moved by an argument that has strong political appeal but no proper place in a reasoned judicial opinion. Because [the law] recognizes the defendant's right to introduce all mitigating evidence that may inform the jury about his character, the Court suggests

FROM THE BENCH

Payne v. Tennessee, 501 U.S. 808 (1991)

[F]or the jury to assess meaningfully the defendant's moral culpability and blameworthiness, it should have before it at the sentencing phase evidence of the specific harm caused by the defendant. "[T]he State has a legitimate interest in counteracting the mitigating evidence which the defendant is entitled to put in, by reminding the sentencer that just as the murderer should be considered as an individual, so too the victim is an individual whose death represents a unique loss to society and in particular to his family." ... [T]urning the victim into a "faceless stranger at the penalty phase of a capital trial" ... may prevent the jury from having before it all the information necessary to determine the proper punishment for a first-degree murder.

The present case is an example of the potential for such unfairness. The capital sentencing jury heard testimony from Payne's girlfriend that they met at church; that he was affectionate, caring, and kind to her children; that he was not an abuser of drugs or alcohol; and that it was inconsistent with his character to have committed the murders. Payne's parents testified that he was a good son, and a clinical psychologist testified that Payne was an extremely polite prisoner and suffered from a low IQ.... In contrast, the only evidence of the impact of Payne's offenses ... was Nicholas' grandmother's description ... that the child misses his mother and baby sister.... [T]here is nothing unfair about allowing the jury to bear in mind that harm at the same time as it considers the mitigating evidence introduced by the defendant. The Supreme Court of Tennessee ... said: "It is an that fairness requires that the State be allowed to respond with similar evidence about the victim. . . . This argument is a classic non sequitur: The victim is not on trial; her character, whether good or bad, cannot therefore constitute either an aggravating or a mitigating circumstance. . . .

The Constitution grants certain rights to the criminal defendant and imposes special limitations on the State designed to protect the individual from overreaching by the disproportionately powerful State.[3]

---

affront to the civilized members of the human race to say that at sentencing in a capital case, a parade of witnesses may praise the background, character and good deeds of Defendant (as was done in this case), without limitation as to relevancy, but nothing may be said that bears upon the character of, or the harm imposed, upon the victims."

...Under the aegis of the Eighth Amendment, we have given the broadest latitude to the defendant to introduce relevant mitigating evidence reflecting on his individual personality, and the defendant's attorney may argue that evidence to the jury. Petitioner's attorney in this case did just that. For the reasons discussed above, we now reject the view ... that a State may not permit the prosecutor to similarly argue to the jury the human cost of the crime of which the defendant stands convicted. We reaffirm the view expressed by Justice Cardozo in *Snyder v. Massachusetts*, 291 U.S. 97, 122 (1934): "[J]ustice, though due to the accused, is due to the accuser also. The concept of fairness must not be strained till it is narrowed to a filament. We are to keep the balance true."

We thus hold that if the State chooses to permit the admission of victim impact evidence and prosecutorial argument on that subject, the Eighth Amendment erects no per se bar. A State may legitimately conclude that evidence about the victim and about the impact of the murder on the victim's family is relevant to the jury's decision as to whether or not the death penalty should be imposed. There is no reason to treat such evidence differently than other relevant evidence is treated.

The jury selection process is unfair to defendants.

Jurors are chosen from a pool of potential jurors called the *venire* in a process called *voir dire*. In criminal trials, prosecutors try to exclude jurors whom they feel are more likely to find the defendant not guilty; defense attorneys similarly try to exclude jurors thought more likely to convict. Many believe that people from minority groups are less likely to convict than whites; however, because it is illegal to exclude jurors solely because of their race, prosecutors often look for other rationales to exclude jurors. This often requires extensive questioning about a variety of issues, such as whether a potential juror has been a crime victim.

During the voir dire for capital trials, prosecutors engage in a process called death qualification. The prosecution is able to exclude any juror who says that he or she would not be willing to impose the death penalty if selected as a juror; the U.S. Supreme Court upheld this practice in *Witherspoon v. Illinois* (1968). While holding that people cannot be excluded from a jury for simply expressing general misgivings about capital punishment, the Court held that potential jurors *can* be excluded for specifically saying that they could not apply the death penalty to the defendant in that particular case. In *Witherspoon*, the condemned prisoner had claimed:

> [A jury that has been "death-qualified"], unlike one chosen at random from a cross-section of the community, must necessarily be biased in favor of conviction, for the kind of juror who would be unperturbed by the prospect of sending a man to his death . . . is the kind of juror who would too readily ignore the presumption of the defendant's innocence . . . and return a verdict of guilt.[4]

The Court rejected that argument, stating: "We simply cannot conclude . . . that the exclusion of jurors opposed to capital punishment results in an unrepresentative jury on the issue of guilt or substantially increases the risk of conviction."[5]

Critics of the death penalty dispute the Court's conclusion in *Witherspoon* and strongly believe that excluding potential jurors who would not impose the death penalty violates a defendant's constitutional rights. Houston attorney Clay S. Conrad blames this aspect of the jury selection process for increasing the amount of time that it takes to select capital juries. It also ends up removing a larger percentage of women and minorities compared to white men, since women and minorities are often less supportive of the death penalty. "That may explain why capital juries are approximately 43 percent more likely to sentence a killer to die if his victim is white," Conrad noted. The result of this is that capital juries "are not only biased towards death (instead of life imprisonment), but conviction," too, and that of the thousands of inmates on death row, "not a single one has received a trial before a jury representative of the community. . . ."[6]

Public pressure plays too great a role in capital punishment.

Although the Constitution guarantees the accused the right to a fair trial and freedom from cruel and unusual punishment, public pressure plays a role—too great a role, abolitionists say—in determining whether a district attorney will seek the death penalty in any given case. Because district attorneys are either elected officials or political appointees, public satisfaction does play a role in whether they keep their jobs.

Even though jury deliberations are supposed to remain secret, many times a jury feels public pressure to enforce the death penalty. Because of the widespread public misconception that murderers frequently are released after serving very little time, members of the jury do not want to be blamed for returning a vicious killer to the streets. Because of public pressure, abolitionists argue, a sentence of death is often not the result of a fair trial.

Worse, because public pressure often depends on the race of the accused or the victim, the effect of uneven public pressure is uneven application of the death penalty. Unfortunately, incidents show that racism often plays a role in the decision of whether to convict and whether to sentence someone to death. For example, in August 1980, 16-year-old Cheryl Fergeson, the manager of a visiting girls' volleyball team, was raped and murdered inside a Conroe, Texas, high school while a volleyball game was being played outside. The community demanded that the perpetrator be brought to justice, and put great pressure on law enforcement officials. Parents even threatened to keep their children home from school. When Clarence Brandley, an African-American man, was arrested and first brought to trial, he faced an all-white jury in a county that was only about 5 percent African American. There was very little evidence against Brandley, but the jury voted 11 to 1 for conviction. William Srack, the juror who dissented, was called a "nigger lover" by his fellow jurors and received threatening and harassing phone calls for months afterward. At a second trial, Brandley was convicted and sentenced to death by an all-white jury.

Innocent people have been sentenced to death.

Today Clarence Brandley is a free man: More than a decade after the crime, all charges were dropped. Despite strong evidence that someone else had committed the crime, Brandley had come within six days of execution. Abolitionists cite cases like Brandley's to support their argument that all of the legal safeguards that a defendant has on paper can break down in the real-life court room, resulting in innocent people being condemned to death.

Brandley was the supervisor of the janitorial staff at Conroe High School, and he also happened to be the only African-American member of the staff. When Brandley and another janitor found Fergeson's body, suspicion began to focus on Brandley almost immediately. According to the testimony of the other janitor, a police officer said to them, "One of you two is going to hang for this," and then said to Brandley, "Since you're the nigger, you're elected."[7] The first trial ended in a hung jury because of the dissent of juror Srack (whom Jesse Jackson observes "almost became a hung juror,"[8] quite literally). Brandley was then convicted at the second trial.

The evidence at the second trial was conflicting. Circumstantial evidence pointed to Brandley. Other janitors had testified seeing Brandley headed toward the bathroom where Fergeson had last been seen. During the search, Brandley told the other janitors to meet him at another building but did not meet them for 45 minutes. During the search for Fergeson, Brandley asked another janitor to search the loft in which the girl's body was found, not once, but three times—after the first two searches failed to discover her body concealed under a piece of plywood. However, although this circumstantial evidence pointed to Brandley, there was no physical evidence linking him to the crime. Several red hairs—which could not have belonged to either Fergeson or Brandley—were found on her body. The second jury convicted Brandley in 1981, but when he attempted to appeal his conviction, physical evidence, including hair and semen samples, had been destroyed or discarded.

With missing physical evidence and the circumstantial evidence implicating him, Brandley's appeals were fruitless. His first break came in 1986, when a woman from a nearby town—who claimed to have heard nothing previously of the crime or the trials—came forward to say that her former common-law husband had told her in 1980 that he had killed a woman, but that she had not believed him until she heard about Fergeson's murder a few years later. Her former husband, James Robinson, had been a janitor at Conroe High and had been fired not long before the murder. Another janitor, Gary Acreman, who had testified at Brandley's trial, took back his testimony and told investigators a new story implicating Robinson. Acreman's nervous, contradictory stories made investigators suspect that Acreman also might have been involved.

Despite the new evidence, Brandley's appeals continued to be unsuccessful until March 1987, when he received a stay of execution only six days before he was scheduled to die. A trial judge, after reviewing the evidence in the case, recommended to the court of criminal appeals in October 1987 that Brandley be given a new trial in another county, where racism and publicity would play less of a role. But Brandley remained on death row for two more years. Finally, in December 1989, the court granted him a new trial, and in January 1990, Clarence Brandley was released on bail after spending nine years in prison. When the U.S. Supreme Court upheld the order of a new trial, the district attorney finally dropped the charges against Brandley in October 1990.

Brandley's case is one of the best-publicized cases of an innocent person spending time on death row. But it is not the only case. A study by abolitionists Hugo Adam Bedau and Michael Radelet published in 1987 in the *Stanford Law Review* uncovered 350 cases in which people were convicted of capital crimes although evidence later indicated that they were innocent. For many, the margin of error might be small, but due to the irreversible nature of the death penalty, any margin of error is too great.

Summary

There are documented cases of innocent people being convicted of crimes and sentenced to death. Even one incident like this is one too many. Abolitionists point to cases like Clarence Brandley's to argue that procedural safeguards are necessary and should be strengthened, not weakened as many pro–death penalty advocates would argue.

Capital Punishment Is Applied Fairly in Our Society

Claims of racial discrimination always grab headlines, but many feel that bringing up race during a trial can divert people's attention from real issues. For example, in the mid 1990s, former football star O.J. Simpson went on trial for the murder of his ex-wife and her boyfriend. Simpson, who is African American, had a large legal team that made great efforts to label the Los Angeles Police Department as racist (his ex-wife and her boyfriend were white).

The not-guilty verdict was widely criticized: Perhaps some, or even many police officers were racist, but did that racism have any bearing on the determination of whether Simpson killed Nicole Brown Simpson and Ronald Goldman? People accused Simpson's defense lawyers of "playing the race card," or diverting attention from real issues by insisting that racism tainted the proceedings. The race card is also frequently played in capital murder trials and appeals. Defense attorneys and abolitionists claim that one of the major problems with capital punishment is that it is applied unfairly to minorities, the poor, and the uneducated. By contrast, death penalty supporters believe that legal safeguards currently in place are sufficient to deter discrimination in sentencing, and that it is unfair to draw broad generalities based on sentences that are specific to each case.

FROM THE BENCH

McCleskey v. Kemp, 481 U.S. 279 (1987)

[A] statistical study performed by Professors David C. Baldus, Charles Pulaski, and George Woodworth (the Baldus study) [indicates that] in Georgia during the 1970s ... defendants charged with killing white persons received the death penalty in 11% of the cases, but defendants charged with killing blacks received the death penalty in only 1% of the cases. [Also] 4% of the black defendants received the death penalty, as opposed to 7% of the white defendants.

Baldus also ... found that the death penalty was assessed in 22% of the cases involving black defendants and white victims; 8% of the cases involving white defendants and white victims; 1% of the cases involving black defendants and black victims; and 3% of the cases involving white defendants and black victims. Similarly, Baldus found that prosecutors sought the death penalty in 70% of the cases involving black defendants and white victims; 32% of the cases involving white defendants and white victims; 15% of the cases involving black defendants and black victims; and 19% of the cases involving white defendants and black victims....

[E]ach particular decision to impose the death penalty is made by a petit jury selected from a properly constituted venire. Each jury is unique in its composition, and the Constitution requires that its decision rest on consideration of innumerable factors that vary according to the characteristics of the individual defendant and the facts of the particular capital offense....

[Georgia's death penalty] statute narrows the class of murders subject to the death penalty to cases in which the jury finds at least one statutory aggravating circumstance beyond a reasonable doubt. Conversely, it allows the defendant to introduce any relevant mitigating evidence that might influence the jury not to impose a death sentence.... The statute requires [the Georgia Supreme Court] to review each sentence to determine whether it was imposed under

The death penalty is not applied in a discriminatory way.

Many abolitionists charge that the death penalty is disproportionately applied to African Americans and the poor, but death penalty supporters dispute this conclusion. The Supreme Court seems to agree with death penalty supporters. In *McCleskey v. Kemp* (1987), the Court rejected a convicted criminal's challenge

the influence of passion or prejudice, whether the evidence supports the jury's finding of a statutory aggravating circumstance, and whether the sentence is disproportionate to sentences imposed in generally similar murder cases. To aid the court's review, the trial judge answers a questionnaire about the trial, including detailed questions as to "the quality of the defendant's representation [and] whether race played a role in the trial."

. . . Even Professor Baldus does not contend that his statistics prove that race enters into any capital sentencing decisions or that race was a factor in McCleskey's particular case. Statistics at most may show only a likelihood that a particular factor entered into some decisions. There is, of course, some risk of racial prejudice influencing a jury's decision in a criminal case. . . .

Because of the risk that the factor of race may enter the criminal justice process, we have engaged in "unceasing efforts" to eradicate racial prejudice from our criminal justice system. . . . Our efforts have been guided by our recognition that "the inestimable privilege of trial by jury . . . is a vital principle, underlying the whole administration of criminal justice," . . . Thus, it is the jury that is a criminal defendant's fundamental "protection of life and liberty against race or color prejudice."

. . . The capital sentencing decision requires the individual jurors to focus their collective judgment on the unique characteristics of a particular criminal defendant. It is not surprising that such collective judgments often are difficult to explain. But the inherent lack of predictability of jury decisions does not justify their condemnation. . . .

In light of the safeguards designed to minimize racial bias in the process, the fundamental value of jury trial in our criminal justice system, and the benefits that discretion provides to criminal defendants, we hold that the Baldus study does not demonstrate a constitutionally significant risk of racial bias affecting the Georgia capital sentencing process.

to Georgia's death penalty statute—a challenge that was based primarily on a statistical study. The study demonstrated that in 2,000 murder cases in Georgia during the 1970s, defendants were sentenced to death in 22 percent of cases involving African-American defendants and white victims, but only in 1 percent of cases involving African-American defendants and African-American victims. By contrast, defendants were sentenced to death in 8 percent of cases involving white defendants and white victims and 3 percent of cases involving white defendants and African-American victims.

Although the raw numbers, on their face, indicated a clear pattern of discrimination, the study analyzed the statistics further. It examined 230 factors other than race that could be used to explain why particular defendants received the death penalty. Once these factors were considered, the study concluded, African-American defendants were only slightly more likely (1.1 times) than white defendants to receive the death penalty. Although the case put to rest, legally speaking, the notion that the application of the death penalty is racially discriminatory, abolitionists continue to use discrimination as a primary basis for their criticisms of the death penalty. But the Court's opinion in *McCleskey* provides a framework for the argument that racial issues do not influence sentencing.

First: The death penalty is applied according to state statutes—statutes that do not discriminate according to race. State legislatures enact death penalty laws to condemn criminals, not to condemn people of any specific race. In fact, legislatures go to great lengths to ensure that death sentences are given out according to very specific, race-neutral guidelines.

Like most death penalty statutes, the Georgia statute applied in *McCleskey* listed specific types of offenses for which the death penalty may be given. McCleskey's sentence was clearly within the guidelines of the law: He was sentenced to death for shooting a police officer in the face during an armed robbery. On its own, either killing a police officer or killing someone during an armed robbery would serve as grounds for imposing the death penalty under the Georgia statute.

Second: Although statistics might be useful in showing a general trend—that a characteristic (such as race) is present in a certain percentage of outcomes (such as death sentences)—statistics cannot prove that a particular factor determined the outcome in any given case. Because other African-American defendants were not sentenced to death, McCleskey could not prove that his race was the cause of his death sentence. Further, the court concluded that the circumstances of McCleskey's case indicated the likelihood that he would have been sentenced to death regardless of his race:

> [H]e cannot base a constitutional claim on an argument that his case differs from other cases in which defendants did receive the death penalty. On automatic appeal, the Georgia Supreme Court found that McCleskey's death sentence was not disproportionate to other death sentences imposed in the State. . . . The court supported this conclusion with an appendix containing citations to 13 cases involving generally similar murders.[1]

Many supporters of the death penalty willingly admit that all flaws cannot be eliminated from the criminal justice system. It seems inescapable that a defendant who can afford expert legal help is less likely to be found guilty in a murder trial, and therefore less likely to be sentenced to death. But what can be done about the inescapable inequality between wealth and poverty? Professor Ernest Van Den Haag, a well-known death penalty supporter, cautions that society must not abandon its quest for justice simply because some people escape justice: "We should not give up justice, or the death penalty, because we cannot extend it as equally to all the guilty as we wish. If we were not to punish one offender because another got away . . . we would give up justice for the sake of equality."[2]

Legal safeguards prevent the execution of the innocent.

Another reason the Court upheld McCleskey's death sentence was that he had been allowed ample opportunity to defend himself from the death penalty through the legal protections given to capital defendants. The U.S. legal system provides many safeguards for defendants charged with a capital offense. Foremost is the discretion allowed to juries:

> Discretion in the criminal justice system offers substantial benefits to the criminal defendant. Not only can a jury decline to impose the death sentence, it can decline to convict or choose to convict of a lesser offense. Whereas decisions against a defendant's interest may be reversed by the trial judge or on appeal, these discretionary exercises of leniency are final and unreviewable.[3]

State laws also provide special protections to capital defendants. Typically, the defendant is appointed a defense team of two or more attorneys, is entitled to a sentencing hearing in front of a jury, and receives an automatic appeal if sentenced to death. As illustrated by cases such as that of Gary Cone—who in 2007 was still appealing his 1982 death sentence for a double homicide committed in 1980—condemned criminals have ample opportunity to appeal their sentences. Therefore, death penalty supporters argue, whether or not a prosecutor or a jury might have been influenced by racial animosity toward a defendant—because of either the defendant's race or the victim's race—the appeals process ensures that any such alleged discrimination can be brought up during the lengthy appeals process.

Death penalty supporters have sharply criticized the 1987 study by Radelet and Bedau that claimed to show that 350 people had been wrongly convicted of capital offenses. Two attorneys with the U.S. Department of Justice published a study the following year refuting the abolitionists' analysis. Of the 350 cases cited, the defendant was sentenced to death in 139 of them, and 23 were executed. But, as the authors of the original study admitted, the conclusions of innocence in these cases were based on evidence gathered outside of the court proceedings. Nobody confessed to the crimes or was convicted of the crimes that led to any of the executions.

Death penalty supporters believe that ever since the death penalty was restored by the 1976 *Gregg* decision, no inarguably innocent person has been executed. It is true that some people are erroneously arrested for crimes that they did not commit, are charged with them, or even are convicted of them and sentenced to death. But, it is also true that the lengthy and comprehensive appeals process has prevented the execution of innocent people.

The ban on executing people with mental retardation will hinder justice.

By 2002, many states had passed laws limiting or banning the execution of people with mental retardation—generally meaning people who score lower than 70 on standardized IQ tests. Other states did not have a similar ban, but instead allowed jurors to consider a defendant's lower mental capacity as an influencing factor that might make them decide to impose a lesser sentence. However, in the case of *Atkins v. Virginia* (2002), the U.S. Supreme Court held that the execution of people with mental retardation violates the Eighth Amendment's ban on cruel and unusual punishment.

Before the Court handed down its decision, many death penalty supporters opposed a total ban on capital punishment for people with very low IQs. This was not because they supported the execution of those whose mental retardation impairs their ability to distinguish right from wrong, but because a constitutional ban would encourage questionable claims of retardation. For example, the Criminal Justice Legal Foundation filed an amicus ("friend of the court") brief supporting the state of Virginia, announcing, "Our participation in this case will be to help assure that cold-blooded murderers are not able to avoid the punishment they have earned with an unsupported claim that they suffer a mental deficiency."[4] In the *Atkins* case itself, a clinical psychologist testifying for the prosecution disputed the defendant's claim of mental retardation. Atkins' crime was particularly brutal:

> After spending the day drinking alcohol and smoking marijuana, petitioner Daryl Renard Atkins and a partner in crime drove to a convenience store, intending to rob a customer. Their victim was Eric Nesbitt, an airman from Langley Air Force Base, whom they abducted, drove to a nearby automated teller machine, and forced to withdraw $200. They then drove him to a deserted area, ignoring his pleas to leave him unharmed. According to the co-conspirator, whose testimony the jury evidently credited, Atkins ordered Nesbitt out of the vehicle and, after he had taken only a few steps, shot him one, two, three, four, five, six, seven, eight times in the thorax, chest, abdomen, arms, and legs. . . . The jury also heard testimony about petitioner's 16 prior felony convictions for robbery, attempted robbery, abduction, use of a firearm, and maiming.[5]

Justice Scalia, in his dissent, wrote:

> This newest invention promises to be more effective than any of the others in turning the process of capital trial into a game. . . . [T]he symptoms of this condition can readily be feigned. And whereas the capital defendant who feigns insanity risks commitment to a mental institution until he can be

Daryl Atkins sits in a courtroom in York, Virginia, during an appeal of his sentence in 2005. Atkins's first trial led to the U.S. Supreme Court case that barred execution of the mentally retarded.

cured (and then tried and executed) . . . the capital defendant who feigns mental retardation risks nothing at all. The mere pendency of the present case has brought us petitions by death row inmates claiming for the first time, after multiple habeas petitions, that they are retarded.[6]

Many death penalty supporters share Justice Scalia's concern that false claims of mental retardation will clog up the court system. When the decision was announced, various estimates suggested that between 150 and 300 convicts already on death row nationwide would be spared from execution as a result of the ruling. Indeed, in the years since the *Atkins* decision, numerous defendants have raised claims of mental retardation. Determining whether someone is mentally retarded and cannot be executed raises both questions of law (what constitutes retardation) and questions of fact (does this particular defendant meet these criteria)?

For example, Oklahoma death row inmate Karl Lee Myers, who had already appealed his case all the way to the U.S. Supreme Court, raised another appeal after the *Atkins* decision was announced, seeking to overturn his death sentence by claiming that he is mentally retarded. A judge granted Myers a jury trial, which took 10 days, and the jury found that he was not mentally retarded. Myers then appealed that decision to the Oklahoma Court of Criminal Appeals, which denied his appeal, noting:

> Myers had held a regular job as a truck driver, and had successfully passed the test for a commercial driver's license allowing him to drive a tractor-trailer rig. He had also worked as a forklift operator in a warehouse, loading and unloading trucks based on bills of lading. That job required him to complete classroom training, proficiency training, and pass a written test in order to drive the forklift. He was also able to do some work as a mechanic and worked for a time in an automotive shop. While in prison, Myers learned to read simple material and earned a certificate showing he had learned to weld and fabricate metal.

Myers lived by himself and was able to maintain his home and take care of himself and several animals. Myers assisted in the care of his wife as she was dying of cancer. He was capable enough to follow directions and retrieve needed medication and supplies. After his wife died, Myers managed his own financial affairs, including refinancing his property.

Myers was able to effectively communicate with people. He was able to socialize with acquaintances without difficulty. Myers could understand others, make himself understood, express his wishes, and understand the reactions of others. He was able to plan for future events. He was able to mislead people and, when confronted with inconsistencies in his stories, he could conform his story to fit the facts.[7]

Throughout the trial and appeal, Myers was represented by court-appointed attorneys, further drawing upon public resources.

The Supreme Court's exclusion of mentally retarded defendants from the death penalty means that courts can no longer determine on a case-by-case basis whether someone understood the nature and seriousness of the crime and therefore could be considered worthy of a sentence of death. In a law review article, Dora Klein takes issue with the Court's conclusion that people who are mentally retarded "by definition have diminished capacities to understand and process information, . . . to abstract from mistakes and learn from experience, to engage in logical reasoning, to control impulses, and to understand the reactions of others."[8] Instead, she argues, people who are mentally retarded have a wide variety of abilities and disabilities. She criticizes the Court's "absolutist position that mentally retarded offenders 'by definition' possess certain traits that make them less culpable than offenders who are not mentally retarded."[9] Her point is that the Supreme Court wrongly lumped all people who are mentally retarded into a single category of being unable to understand the nature of their crimes.

Banning the execution of mentally ill defendants will raise similar concerns.

The Supreme Court has long held that the Constitution prohibits the execution of a legally insane defendant, meaning "a person who has no comprehension of why he has been singled out and stripped of his fundamental right to life."[10] Many people suffer from serious mental illnesses, such as schizophrenia, that cause them to have irrational beliefs; for example, one might have delusions of being the object of a government conspiracy. Mental health advocates have suggested that people who suffer from serious mental illnesses should not be executed.

For example, the American Bar Association (the nation's largest organization of lawyers) adopted a policy opposing the death penalty for certain people who have a "severe mental disorder" that impairs their ability "to conform their conduct to the requirements of the law," including those "who intended to commit the crime and knew that the conduct was wrongful, but experienced confusion and self-referential thinking that prevented them from recognizing its full ramifications."[11] Some advocates go further, like Laura Izutsu, whose 2005 law review article calls for "a categorical exemption from capital punishment for individuals with severe mental disorders,"[12] which she defines to include schizophrenia, schizoaffective disorder (which is similar to schizophrenia), and bipolar disorder (or manic depression).

In a 2007 case involving convicted murderer Scott Panetti, the Supreme Court took a step toward excluding people with serious mental illnesses from death row. Panetti has been diagnosed variously with schizophrenia and other mental disorders. When on his medication, he is able to function well, but when he does not take his medications, he suffers from irrational beliefs. After stopping his medications in 1992, Panetti dressed in camouflage, armed himself with several weapons, and went to his in-laws' house, where his wife and daughter were staying after obtaining a protective order to keep Panetti away. He held his wife, daughter, and his wife's parents at gunpoint, and then shot his in-laws, spraying his wife and daughter with blood.

Before his 1995 trial, Panetti refused to take medications to control his schizophrenia, and then he insisted upon representing

FROM THE BENCH

Panetti v. Quarterman, 551 U.S. ___ (2007) (Thomas, J., Dissenting)

In a 2007 decision, the U.S. Supreme Court sent the case of Scott Panetti, a man who has schizophrenia and represented himself in court wearing a cowboy outfit, back to the lower courts for a determination as to whether he could understand why he was being executed, directing that he not be executed if he could not understand the purpose of the punishment. Justice Thomas, joined by Justices Scalia and Alito and Chief Justice Roberts, dissented.

Scott Panetti's mental problems date from at least 1981. While Panetti's mental illness may make him a sympathetic figure, state and federal courts have repeatedly held that he is competent to face the consequences of the two murders he committed. In a competency hearing prior to his trial in 1995, a jury determined that Panetti was competent to stand trial. A judge then determined that Panetti was competent to represent himself. At his trial, the jury rejected Panetti's insanity defense, which was supported by the testimony of two psychiatrists. Since the trial, both state and federal habeas courts have rejected Panetti's claims that he was incompetent to stand trial and incompetent to waive his right to counsel.

This case should be simple. Panetti brings a claim under *Ford v. Wainwright*, 477 U.S. 399 (1986), that he is incompetent to be executed. Presented for the first time in Panetti's second federal habeas application, this claim undisputedly does not meet the statutory requirements for filing a "second or successive" habeas application. As such, Panetti's habeas application must be dismissed. Ignoring this clear statutory mandate, the Court bends over backwards to allow Panetti to bring his *Ford* claim despite no evidence that his condition has worsened—or even changed—since 1995. Along the way, the Court improperly refuses to defer to the state court's finding of competency even though Panetti had the opportunity to submit evidence and to respond to the court-appointed experts' report. Moreover, without undertaking even a cursory Eighth Amendment analysis, the Court imposes a new standard for determining incompetency. I respectfully dissent.

himself. He wore a cowboy outfit to court, complete with "pants that looked like leather suede tucked into his cowboy boots . . . a cowboy style shirt with a bandana . . . [and] a big cowboy hat that hung on a string over his back."[13] During the trial, he attempted to call Jesus, the Pope, and the late President John F. Kennedy as witnesses. A jury convicted him and sentenced him to death for the brutal murders. As he sat on death row and refused to take medications, he continued to be delusional. His lawyer reported that "Panetti believed that his imminent execution was part of a satanic conspiracy to prevent him from preaching the Gospel,"[14] and that Panetti believed that the state of Texas was simply using the murders of his in-laws as a pretext for its true reasons for executing him.

In 2007, the U.S. Supreme Court took up Panetti's appeal, based on his lawyers' argument that Panetti's delusional beliefs made him believe that the execution was unjust, although he did understand why he was sentenced to death. The lower courts had refused to consider this argument, holding that because he understood the facts that led to his sentence, he was legally competent to be executed. The Supreme Court held that the lower courts' approach was too narrow, and it sent the case back to the lower courts to consider Panetti's argument "that he suffers from a severe, documented mental illness that is the source of gross delusions preventing him from comprehending the meaning and purpose of the punishment to which he has been sentenced."[15]

Oddly, the Supreme Court did not spell out a specific legal standard for the lower courts to follow, noting, "We do not attempt to set down a rule governing all competency deter-minations."[16] Instead, the Supreme Court directed the trial court to consider the "conclusions of physicians, psychiatrists, and other experts in the field," which "may clarify the extent to which severe delusions may render a subject's perception of reality so distorted that he should be deemed incompetent."[17]

The Supreme Court pointed to its earlier decisions for use in developing the proper standard: "It is proper to allow the court charged with overseeing the development of the evidentiary record in this case the initial opportunity to resolve petitioner's constitutional claim."[18]

The *Panetti* decision raises concerns among correctional officials, since it suggests that a defendant who understands the wrongness of his or her crime but was delusional could avoid execution. The standard seems to create an incentive for death row inmates with mental illnesses to refuse to take their medications. At issue is not whether the person understood that what he or she did was wrong, but the convict's current state of mind. And this could change if medications are rejected. It also raises the possibility that the condemned will attempt to feign or exaggerate symptoms of mental illnesses in order to escape execution. After the Supreme Court announced its decision in *Panetti*, Texas Solicitor General Ted Cruz, who argued the case, said that the decision "will invite abuse from capital murderers, subject the courts to numerous false claims of incompetency and even further delay justice for the victims' families."[19]

Summary

Although one of the most enduring criticisms of capital punishment is that it is applied unfairly, supporters of the death penalty argue that many safeguards are in place to make sure that death sentences are handed down in an equitable way. They say that when similar crimes are compared, there is no pattern of racism in sentencing. Additionally, people can only be sentenced to death if convicted of a capital crime, and once convicted, the appeals process allows for overturning wrongful convictions. Although some people who have been sentenced to death have had their convictions overturned, there is no credible evidence that an innocent person has been executed since the Supreme Court reinstated the death penalty in a 1976 ruling. If anything, supporters say, the legal protections against the death penalty are too broad, and categorical exclusions of mentally retarded and mentally ill defendants from the death penalty allow people to manipulate the system to escape punishment.

Capital Punishment Is Applied Unfairly in Our Society

Regardless of the Supreme Court's 1987 decision in *McCleskey v. Kemp*, abolitionists believe that the death penalty continues to be applied in a discriminatory way. In the words of Richard Dieter, executive director of the Death Penalty Information Center, "From . . . slavery . . . through the years of lynchings and Jim Crow laws, capital punishment has always been deeply affected by race. Unfortunately, the days of racial bias in the death penalty are not a remnant of the past."[1] One of the so-called reforms of the French Revolution was that members of the upper and lower classes were executed by the same method; centuries later in the United States, the death penalty is reserved almost exclusively for the poorest defendants. And although the Supreme Court recently barred the execution of people with mental retardation, abolitionists firmly believe that the most vulnerable defendants are still the ones to receive the death penalty.

Race plays too large a role in sentencing.

In some cases like Clarence Brandley's—in which a police investigator told him, "Since you're the nigger, you're elected" to hang for the crime—racism plays an obvious role. However, in many other cases, racism plays perhaps a subtler role. The study at issue in *McCleskey* clearly indicates that the death penalty is handed out in a way that disproportionately affects African-American defendants, as well as defendants convicted of killing white victims. More recent studies confirm this: According to the Death Penalty Information Center, African-American defendants in Philadelphia are nearly four times as likely to receive a death sentence as are white defendants in similar cases, and nationally, 98 percent of district attorneys are white in those counties that have the death penalty. Overall, the organization says, "Examinations of [racial bias] have now been conducted in every major death penalty state. In 96% of these reviews, there was a pattern of either race-of-victim or race-of-defendant discrimination, or both."[2]

One way to eliminate racial discrepancies in sentencing, some abolitionists suggest, is to strictly limit the crimes for which the death penalty may be given. In his dissent in *McCleskey*, Justice Stevens noted:

> [T]here exist certain categories of extremely serious crimes for which prosecutors consistently seek, and juries consistently impose, the death penalty without regard to the race of the victim or the race of the offender. If Georgia were to narrow the class of death-eligible defendants to those categories, the danger of arbitrary and discriminatory imposition of the death penalty would be significantly decreased, if not eradicated.[3]

It is important to note that some death penalty supporters also favor limiting the death penalty to the most serious of crimes.

Poverty plays too large a role in sentencing.

In addition to the racist views that can—consciously or unconsciously—influence prosecutors, judges, and jurors, many abolitionists believe, like Hugo Adam Bedau, that the death penalty is tainted by "[d]iscrimination against the poor (and in our society, racial minorities are disproportionately poor)."[4] Organizations opposing the death penalty, such as the American Civil Liberties Union (ACLU) cite inadequate legal representation as a key factor in determining whether a defendant is sentenced to death in murder cases. Defendants who cannot afford a lawyer are entitled to legal representation; however, court-appointed lawyers are overworked and underpaid. According to the ACLU, a lawyer cannot earn a living representing lower-income defendants in capital trials, and lawyers might even lose money by taking these kinds of cases: "In some jurisdictions the hourly rates for appointed attorneys are less than the minimum wage, and usually much less than the lawyer's hourly expenses."[5]

Because the pay for court-appointed lawyers is so low, and the cases require so much time to prepare adequately, many people are sentenced to death after being represented by lawyers who are often inexperienced and unprepared for the complexities of a capital trial. The ACLU criticizes the lack of funding for court-appointed defense attorneys, investigators, and expert witnesses "in the face of the almost limitless . . . funding for the prosecution," and concludes that the lack of funding results in a death penalty that discriminates against the poor: "Wealthy people who can hire their own counsel are generally spared the death penalty, no matter how heinous their crimes. Poor people do not have the same opportunity to buy their lives."[6]

An example used by abolitionists to highlight the problems with court-appointed counsels is the case of Ronald Frye. Living in poverty and addicted to crack, Frye was appointed two lawyers to defend him from charges that he stabbed his landlord after the landlord gave Frye an eviction notice. Frye's crime was

FROM THE BENCH

McCleskey v. Kemp, 481 U.S. 279 (1987) (Brennan, J., Dissenting)

At some point in this case, Warren McCleskey doubtless asked his lawyer whether a jury was likely to sentence him to die. A candid reply to this question would have been disturbing. First, counsel would have to tell McCleskey that few of the details of the crime or of McCleskey's past criminal conduct were more important than the fact that his victim was white.... Furthermore, counsel would feel bound to tell McCleskey that defendants charged with killing white victims in Georgia are 4.3 times as likely to be sentenced to death as defendants charged with killing blacks.... In addition, frankness would compel the disclosure that it was more likely than not that the race of McCleskey's victim would determine whether he received a death sentence: 6 of every 11 defendants convicted of killing a white person would not have received the death penalty if their victims had been black ... while, among defendants with aggravating and mitigating factors comparable to McCleskey's, 20 of every 34 would not have been sentenced to die if their victims had been black.... Finally, the assessment would not be complete without the information that cases involving black defendants and white victims are more likely to result in a death sentence than cases featuring any other racial combination of defendant and victim.... The story could be told in a variety of ways, but McCleskey could not fail to grasp [that] there was a significant chance that race would play a prominent role in determining if he lived or died....

The Baldus study indicates that, after taking into account some 230 nonracial factors that might legitimately influence a sentencer, the jury more likely than not would have spared McCleskey's life had his victim been black. [In cases] in which the jury has considerable discretion in choosing a sentence ... death is imposed in 34% of white-victim crimes and 14% of black-victim crimes, a difference of 139% in the rate of imposition of the death penalty.... In other words, just under 59%—almost 6 in 10—defendants comparable to McCleskey would not have received the death penalty if their victims had been black.

Furthermore, even examination of the sentencing system as a whole, factoring in those cases in which the jury exercises little discretion, indicates the influence of race on capital sentencing. For the Georgia system as a whole ... death is imposed in 11% of all white-victim cases, [and] the rate in comparably aggravated black-victim cases is 5%. The rate of capital sentencing in a white-victim case is thus 120% greater than the rate in a black-victim case. Put another way, over half—55%—of defendants in white-victim crimes in Georgia would not have been sentenced to die if their victims had been black. Of the more than 200 variables potentially relevant to a sentencing decision, race of the victim is a powerful explanation for variation in death sentence rates—as powerful as nonracial aggravating factors such as a prior murder conviction or acting as the principal planner of the homicide.

These adjusted figures are only the most conservative indication of the risk that race will influence the death sentences of defendants in Georgia. Data unadjusted for the mitigating or aggravating effect of other factors show an even more pronounced disparity by race. The capital sentencing rate for all white-victim cases was almost 11 times greater than the rate for black-victim cases.... Furthermore, blacks who kill whites are sentenced to death at nearly 22 times the rate of blacks who kill blacks, and more than 7 times the rate of whites who kill blacks.... In addition, prosecutors seek the death penalty for 70% of black defendants with white victims, but for only 15% of black defendants with black victims, and only 19% of white defendants with black victims.... Since our decision upholding the Georgia capital sentencing system in [*Gregg v. Georgia*], the State has executed seven persons. All of the seven were convicted of killing whites, and six of the seven executed were black. Such execution figures are especially striking in light of the fact that, during the period encompassed by the Baldus study, only 9.2% of Georgia homicides involved black defendants and white victims, while 60.7% involved black victims. The statistical evidence in this case thus relentlessly documents the risk that McCleskey's sentence was influenced by racial considerations. This evidence shows that there is a better than even chance in Georgia that race will influence the decision to impose the death penalty: a majority of defendants in white-victim crimes would not have been sentenced to die if their victims had been black.... Surely, we should not be willing to take a person's life if the chance that his death sentence was irrationally imposed is more likely than not. In light of the gravity of the interest at stake, petitioner's statistics on their face are a powerful demonstration of the type of risk that our Eighth Amendment jurisprudence has consistently condemned.

brutal, but there was some question as to his lawyers' competence during the proceedings. Although Frye appealed his death sentence based on claims that his court-appointed attorneys had not represented him effectively, his appeal was denied. The state of North Carolina executed him by lethal injection on August 31, 2001.

At Frye's trial, the defense attorneys had called an expert witness to discuss Frye's mental state. In discussions with this clinical psychologist:

> Frye recounted a particularly troubled personal history: at the age of four, he was given away at a restaurant by his parents to a family of strangers; he was severely beaten and subjected to extreme physical torture by the father of that family; subsequently, he had lived in several foster homes. Later, as a teenager, Frye dropped out of high school and abused drugs.[7]

The psychologist further testified at the trial that "Frye suffered from paranoia, mixed substance abuse, mixed personality, child abuse syndrome . . . [and a] diminished capacity to know right from wrong. . . ."[8] However, because Frye did not want to involve his family in the trial, the defense attorneys never presented any direct evidence of his abandonment, extreme abuse (including being whipped with a bullwhip), or any other details of a youth filled with abuse, poverty, and drugs. (The psychologist's testimony did not definitively establish abuse because he did not witness the abuse.)

More disturbingly, one of Frye's attorneys abused alcohol throughout the time that he was representing Frye. Although the attorney later was forced to withdraw from another capital case, the federal court that heard Frye's appeal did not find the attorney's alcohol abuse grounds for overturning the death sentence:

> We are indeed troubled by [the attorney's] acknowledgment of a decades-long routine of drinking approximately twelve

ounces of rum each evening. However, the district court found that [he] "never consumed alcohol during the work day and never performed any work on the case when he had consumed alcohol." . . . We agree with our sister circuits that, in order for an attorney's alcohol addiction to make his assistance constitutionally ineffective, there must be specific instances of deficient performance attributable to alcohol.[9]

Unlike the Texas inmate whose death sentence was overturned because his lawyer had slept through parts of the trial, Frye was not so lucky. Unfortunately, say death penalty opponents, most capital defendants simply do not receive adequate legal help.

Abolitionists won a victory with *Atkins v. Virginia*, when the Supreme Court banned the execution of people with mental retardation. Much of the court's reasoning was based on the unique challenges faced by mentally retarded defendants, such as the danger of "false confessions" and a "demeanor [that] may create an unwarranted impression of lack of remorse for their crimes."[10] However, some of the rationales used by the court could just as easily apply to other groups. Minorities who are subject to discrimination might also have a "lesser ability . . . to make a persuasive showing of mitigation in the face of prosecutorial evidence of one or more aggravating factors."[11] Similarly, people who lack education might also be "less able to give meaningful assistance to their counsel," and "typically [be] poor witnesses."[12]

Another reason why the *Atkins* decision might give some hope to abolitionists is that because of an overall pattern of discrimination, the Court struck down the death penalty as applied to an entire group of defendants. This seems to be a major change in philosophy from the *McCleskey* decision, which rejected evidence of widespread race-related differences in sentencing as a rationale for overturning McCleskey's death sentence.

In fact, the Supreme Court has extended the logic of *Atkins* to establish another category of defendants who cannot face the death penalty: people who committed their crimes while under the age of 18. In *Roper v. Simmons,* the Court noted of youthful offenders: "Their own vulnerability and comparative lack of control over their immediate surroundings mean juveniles have a greater claim than adults to be forgiven for failing to escape negative influences in their whole environment."[13]

Capital punishment diverts money from crime prevention.

Another way that the death penalty discriminates against the poor, minorities, and other vulnerable groups is that the high cost of trying capital cases diverts money from the root causes of crime. Not only are people in lower income and certain minority groups more likely to be convicted of a crime, but they also are frequently victims of crime. Sadly, say abolitionists, the high costs of enforcing the death penalty—as opposed to prison sentences—mean that the criminal justice system is using resources that it could be using to fight crime. Many jurisdictions have, in fact, reduced the size of their police forces while continuing to impose the death penalty.

A report by the Death Penalty Information Center based on nationwide surveys found that even law enforcement officials— to a large extent—think that the death penalty is not working, and that society should take the millions of dollars spent each year on enforcing the death penalty and devote it to crime prevention measures. The report cites resolutions passed by various law enforcement and anti-crime organizations: "Rarely is the death penalty even mentioned in their discussions. Instead, the solutions are changes and programs that affect a broad range of people and go to the roots of why violent crime has become so prevalent."[14]

Among the most effective crime prevention techniques cited by the study were increased numbers of police officers; "community policing," including more officers on foot patrol; offering drug treatment programs to anyone who needs them; creating separate drug courts to handle minor offenses; addressing family violence; reducing high school dropout rates; teaching conflict resolution skills in schools; reducing unemployment; enacting tougher anti-gang laws; and removing illegal handguns from the streets.

The *Atkins* ban on executing mentally retarded defendants has been weakened by state court rulings.

Death penalty supporters have criticized the *Atkins* decision, which categorically prohibits the death penalty for mentally retarded defendants, as having the potential to burden the court systems. But abolitionists say the opposite is true. Rather than having a fair opportunity to demonstrate that they are mentally retarded and thus exempt from consideration for the death penalty, defendants are often given inadequate consideration by state courts.

For example, the Supreme Court of Mississippi upheld a lower court's decision to deny William Ray Hughes an opportunity for a hearing to present evidence that he is mentally retarded. In his efforts to get a hearing on his claim, Hughes submitted an affidavit from a psychologist that his IQ was in a range that indicated mental retardation. Still, the court denied the claim because it felt that the psychologist was unqualified. As the court noted:

> The State noted that [the psychologist's resume] included certification from the American Board of Forensic Examiners, an organization that was sharply criticized as a certification mill in an article entitled "Expertise to Go" written by Mark Hansen which appeared in the American Bar Association's eJournal in February 2000.[15]

Agreeing with the lower court, the Supreme Court noted that although Hughes "consistently received failing grades in high school before he dropped out," he was not enrolled in special education classes, and that "an affidavit from his employer indicates that Hughes was a model employee."[16] Taking into account the qualifications of the psychologist and Hughes's school and work records, the court noted: "Hughes has technically complied with the requirements for an evidentiary hearing. . . . Notwithstanding the technical compliance, the evidence of record in this case overwhelmingly belies the assertions that Hughes is mentally retarded."[17]

Mental health professionals Ernie Poortinga and Melvin Guyer sharply criticized the court's decision in *Hughes*. They write: "By allowing the appellate judges to decide the factual merits of claims of mental retardation, rather than to permit evidentiary hearings of those claims, the Mississippi Supreme Court appears to reach a result-driven outcome in mental retardation capital case appeals."[18] In other words, Poortinga and Guyer accuse the court of arranging a situation unfair to defendants claiming to be mentally retarded, rather than giving them a fair chance to prove their claims.

Part of the problem, Poortinga and Guyer argue, is that the U.S. Supreme Court's *Atkins* decision announced a stern rule against executing people who are mentally retarded, but left it to the states to define mental retardation and determine how to evaluate claims of it. Poortinga and Guyer write: "The U.S. Supreme Court gave virtually no guidance in setting procedures and guidelines for the factual determination of mental retardation and its resultant exemption from the death penalty."[19] The American Civil Liberties Union argues that the *Atkins* decision was long overdue because the international community has already rejected executing people who are mentally retarded. However, an ACLU report notes that, "[b]ecause of the Supreme Court's failure to clearly articulate a definition of mental retardation, many states continue to allow the execution of people who likely are mentally retarded. These executions are particularly repugnant to many in the international community."[20]

Similar logic supports a ban on executing mentally ill defendants.

Almost as soon as the *Atkins* decision was announced, abolitionists began calling for the decision to be extended to people with serious mental illnesses. Abolitionists and mental health advocates argue that people with illnesses such as schizophrenia often cannot control their actions or appreciate the nature of their wrongdoing, cannot contribute meaningfully to their defense, and cannot be deterred from crimes or repent for wrongdoing. Thus, critics argue, executing mentally ill defendants is unfair and serves no purpose.

Some saw Scott Panetti's case as an opportunity to expand *Atkins'* logic to people with serious mental illnesses. Panetti was suffering from schizophrenia, and thought that the state of Texas was using his conviction of murdering his in-laws as an excuse for its real reason for wanting to execute him: to stop him from preaching the gospel. The Court did not announce a blanket prohibition against executing people with mental illnesses, instead noting:

It might be said that capital punishment is imposed because it has the potential to make the offender recognize at last the gravity of his crime and to allow the community as a whole, including the surviving family and friends of the victim, to affirm its own judgment that the culpability of the prisoner is so serious that the ultimate penalty must be sought and imposed. The potential for a prisoner's recognition of the severity of the offense and the objective of community vindication are called in question, however, if the prisoner's mental state is so distorted by a mental illness that his awareness of the crime and punishment has little or no relation to the understanding of those concepts shared by the community as a whole.[21]

In essence, the execution of people with serious mental illnesses is prohibited only if the person cannot comprehend why he or she is being executed, since it is senseless to punish someone incapable of understanding the purpose of the punishment.

The Justice Project, a criminal justice reform organization, applauded the U.S. Supreme Court's decision to give Panetti a

FROM THE BENCH

Roper v. Simmons, 543 U.S. 551 (2005)

A majority of States have rejected the imposition of the death penalty on juvenile offenders under 18, and we now hold this is required by the Eighth Amendment....

Capital punishment must be limited to those offenders who commit "a narrow category of the most serious crimes" and whose extreme culpability makes them "the most deserving of execution."...There are a number of crimes that beyond question are severe in absolute terms, yet the death penalty may not be imposed for their commission [such as] rape of an adult woman...[and] felony murder where defendant did not kill, attempt to kill, or intend to kill. The death penalty may not be imposed on certain classes of offenders, such as juveniles under 16, the insane, and the mentally retarded, no matter how heinous the crime....These rules vindicate the underlying principle that the death penalty is reserved for a narrow category of crimes and offenders.

Three general differences between juveniles under 18 and adults demonstrate that juvenile offenders cannot with reliability be classified among the worst offenders. First...lack of maturity and an underdeveloped sense of responsibility...often result in impetuous and ill-considered actions and decisions.... In recognition of the comparative immaturity and irresponsibility of juveniles, almost every State prohibits those under 18 years of age from voting, serving on juries, or marrying without parental consent....

The second area of difference is that juveniles are more vulnerable or susceptible to negative influences and outside pressures, including peer pressure....

The third broad difference is that the character of a juvenile is not as well formed as that of an adult. The personality traits of juveniles are more transitory, less fixed....

Once the diminished culpability of juveniles is recognized, it is evident that the penological justifications for the death penalty apply to them with lesser force than to adults. We have held there are two distinct social purposes served by the chance to present evidence of his legal incompetence and possibly overturn his death sentence. The organization noted the fundamental unfairness of putting such a person on trial for his or her life:

death penalty: [retribution and deterrence].... As for retribution, we remarked in *Atkins* that "[i]f the culpability of the average murderer is insufficient to justify the most extreme sanction available to the State, the lesser culpability of the mentally retarded offender surely does not merit that form of retribution."...The same conclusions follow from the lesser culpability of the juvenile offender. Whether viewed as an attempt to express the community's moral outrage or as an attempt to right the balance for the wrong to the victim, the case for retribution is not as strong with a minor as with an adult. Retribution is not proportional if the law's most severe penalty is imposed on one whose culpability or blameworthiness is diminished, to a substantial degree, by reason of youth and immaturity.

As for deterrence, it is unclear whether the death penalty has a significant or even measurable deterrent effect on juveniles.... Here ... the absence of evidence of deterrent effect is of special concern because the same characteristics that render juveniles less culpable than adults suggest as well that juveniles will be less susceptible to deterrence. In particular ... the likelihood that the teenage offender has made the kind of cost-benefit analysis that attaches any weight to the possibility of execution is so remote as to be virtually nonexistent.... To the extent the juvenile death penalty might have residual deterrent effect, it is worth noting that the punishment of life imprisonment without the possibility of parole is itself a severe sanction, in particular for a young person....

Drawing the line at 18 years of age is subject, of course, to the objections always raised against categorical rules. The qualities that distinguish juveniles from adults do not disappear when an individual turns 18. By the same token, some under 18 have already attained a level of maturity some adults will never reach.... However, a line must be drawn.... The age of 18 is the point where society draws the line for many purposes between childhood and adulthood. It is, we conclude, the age at which the line for death eligibility ought to rest.

Ruling halts execution of 72 offenders

The Supreme Court has ruled it's unconstitutional to execute juvenile killers. The ruling overturns death sentences for 72 juvenile offenders currently on death row.

Current age requirements for death penalty by state

Age 16   17   (Number shows offenders currently on death row)

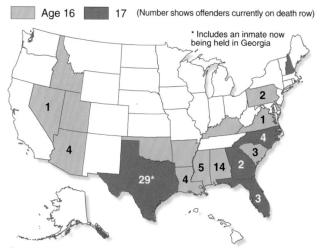

* Includes an inmate now being held in Georgia

States in white either have no death penalty or an age requirement of 18. States with no figure have no juveniles on death row.

SOURCE: Death Penalty Information Center   AP

In *Roper v. Simmons,* the Supreme Court declared the execution of juveniles to be unconstitutional. As a result, the executions of 72 offenders across the United States were halted.

Medical experts who have examined Scott agree that he is severely mentally ill and cannot understand how "this insane man" was permitted to defend himself at trial. Some psychiatrists who had treated Scott during his forced hospitalizations also observed him defend himself at trial. Dr. F.E. Seale said that he "not only thought Scott was incompetent, but, that it was not moral to have him stand trial. It was terribly wrong. I did not know that our legal system would allow an insane man to represent himself in his own trial."[22]

In a law review article, Laurie Izutsu argues that, as with people who are mentally retarded, the deterrent value of capital punishment is lost on people with serious mental illnesses:

> Whereas someone with mental retardation might not refrain from committing an offense because his or her intellectual functioning does not allow that person to see beyond the act to the possibility of penalty, the individual with schizophrenia might also not refrain from committing an offense because of cognitive dysfunction or firmly held erroneous beliefs that lead the defendant to think that he or she is acting in accordance with reality.[23]

Additionally, she writes, death penalty laws take into account a number of factors that give judges and juries a sense of how much responsibility someone should take for his or her actions. For example, a judge or jury might consider evidence that a person was abused as a child. Izutsu argues that people with serious mental illnesses should be held to a lower standard of responsibility for their crimes, and that executing them is unjust: "Justice is also not advanced in terms of retribution, because a person with schizophrenia who commits a capital crime is less morally culpable than a person without schizophrenia."[24]

Summary

Although most abolitionists believe that the death penalty is wrong in all circumstances, many people believe that the uneven way in which the death penalty is administered in the United States is fundamentally unfair. They characterize the system of capital punishment as racist: African-American defendants are much more likely to be sentenced to death, as are people who kill white victims. Poverty is another factor in the unfairness of the death penalty; poor people are provided with lawyers who are too overworked and underprepared to effectively represent their clients. Millions of dollars are spent on the death penalty instead of social programs that could help to prevent crime. And although the U.S. Supreme Court categorically banned the execution of people who are mentally retarded, the states have found ways to deny relief to defendants who claim exemption. Abolitionists hope both to strengthen the prohibition on executing those who are mentally retarded and to expand the ban to those who are seriously mentally ill.

The Future of Capital Punishment in America

What is the future of the death penalty in the United States? Almost everyone—supporters and opponents—agrees that the current system is broken. But people disagree about how to fix it. Many people think that the answer is to eliminate the death penalty entirely, but others believe the opposite—that some of the barriers to execution should in fact be removed. Many people have strongly held beliefs about the death penalty, but others are not so sure how they feel. National opinion polls often produce conflicting results: On the one hand, most people will answer "Yes" if asked whether they support capital punishment. On the other hand, far fewer people answer affirmatively if they are asked whether they would support the death penalty if murderers could be sentenced to life in prison with absolutely no chance of parole.

Support for the death penalty remains high—especially at election time—and many politicians fear taking a strong stand against it. Abolitionists continue to try to influence public opinion by attacking arguments made by death penalty supporters. Increasingly, however, abolitionists seek to educate the public about the existence of laws allowing for life in prison without parole. Their reasoning is that public support of the death penalty is due in large part to people believing that murderers who are sentenced to prison will—like Willie Horton—be released a few years later and commit more crimes.

Whatever a person's position on capital punishment, most people agree that the nation must change the way that the death penalty is administered.

Possible Changes to the Death Penalty in the United States

Despite majority support for the death penalty, many abolitionists remain vigorously dedicated to their cause. The death penalty could be abolished in several ways: crime-by-crime (for example, rape is no longer grounds for the death penalty), state-by-state (a third of states have already abolished the death penalty), or class-by-class (such as abolishing the death penalty for people with serious mental illnesses). Of course, the ultimate goal of abolitionists is for the United States to join other Western industrialized nations in abolishing the death penalty completely. But in order to partially or completely abolish the death penalty, opponents must influence public opinion.

Abolition could be achieved either through the legislature or through the courts. Either way depends on a major shift in public opinion away from support of the death penalty. The U.S. Supreme Court has consistently relied upon "currently prevailing standards of decency" in determining whether a particular application of the death penalty violates the Eighth Amendment's prohibition on cruel and unusual punishment. For example, prevailing attitudes about executing people with mental retardation served as a basis for prohibiting that practice. Certainly, state legislatures will not abolish the death penalty unless public opinion shifts away from support of capital punishment: Politicians depend on votes, and death penalty supporters actively campaign against candidates who oppose capital punishment or want to limit its use.

Reducing the number of crimes for which the death penalty can be given is a measure that has found support from abolitionists, death penalty supporters, and supporters of racial justice alike. It is thought that limiting the death penalty to the most serious and shocking of crimes would eliminate juries' discretion, which often leads to more African-American defendants and more murderers of white victims being sentenced to death. Rather than executing a miniscule percentage of the people who commit potentially capital crimes, stricter guidelines would allow for executing a large percentage of people who are convicted of the worst types of crimes.

But for people who believe that the death penalty is a deterrent to crime, the question that remains is how to deter those crimes that would no longer be punishable by death. Perhaps the answer is to consistently enforce sentences of life in prison without parole. One of the advantages of such sentences is that it actually costs less (according to many estimates) to imprison someone for life than it does to pay for the legal process and the death row incarceration of someone sentenced to death. Without the extra considerations of leniency given to capital defendants and the endless appeals process, the life-without-parole sentences could be enforced more consistently. If criminals knew that being caught for a crime would mean that they would never regain their freedom, they might be more deterred than they would be by a slight chance that they would be executed.

Of course, life without parole does not accomplish the same level of retribution, a result that some victims' families might feel is unfair. Perhaps the answer is to do more for victims' families. Many states have fairly comprehensive victims' rights laws. One possibility for improvement is to require convicted criminals to provide compensation, thus obligating them to work while in prison for life.

International Comparisons

Death penalty opponents frequently compare U.S. homicide rates to those of the United Kingdom, which are much lower despite the fact that the British have abolished the death penalty. Saudi Arabia, however, also has very low crime rates and executes a relatively high number of people, although the number is declining. Saudi Arabia also executes people much sooner after sentencing and uses the spectacle of public beheading with a sword as a warning to would-be criminals. Thus, it is difficult to draw any conclusions from comparing the United States to the United Kingdom and Saudi Arabia because the countries' laws and cultures are so different from each other.

The United Kingdom and other Western nations that have abolished the death penalty also have much stricter limits on gun ownership. Countries that execute more people than the United States, such as Iran and China, do not have the same human rights protections—or decades-long appeals processes—as the United States. But Americans seem unlikely to want to part with either the right to bear arms or their civil liberties.

Perhaps the answer to U.S. crime rates has nothing to do with the death penalty. Many believe that gun control, drug treatment, better schools, and other social programs are much more effective than the death penalty in reducing crime. These programs can be instituted regardless of what type of action is taken on the death penalty. Other nations have lowered their crime rates whether or not they use the death penalty as a tool. The question of how to reduce crime remains a major challenge for scholars, law enforcement officials, and everyday citizens. An ideal solution would be for the nation to reduce crime to the point that the death penalty is no longer needed. But there is a long way to go.

Summary

Despite the high costs and questionable societal effects of the death penalty, public support remains strong in the absence of other solutions for deterring crime and assisting crime victims and their families. Internationally, other Western industrialized nations have abolished the death penalty, but the United States has a much higher crime rate than these nations and is still seeking an answer to reducing crime.

Beginning Legal Research

The goals of each book in the Point/Counterpoint series are not only to give the reader a basic introduction to a controversial issue affecting society, but also to encourage the reader to explore the issue more fully. This Appendix is meant to serve as a guide to the reader in researching the current state of the law as well as exploring some of the public policy arguments as to why existing laws should be changed or new laws are needed.

Although some sources of law can be found primarily in law libraries, legal research has become much faster and more accessible with the advent of the Internet. This Appendix discusses some of the best starting points for free access to laws and court decisions, but surfing the Web will uncover endless additional sources of information. Before you can research the law, however, you must have a basic understanding of the American legal system.

The most important source of law in the United States is the Constitution. Originally enacted in 1787, the Constitution outlines the structure of our federal government, as well as setting limits on the types of laws that the federal government and state governments can enact. Through the centuries, a number of amendments have added to or changed the Constitution, most notably the first 10 amendments, which collectively are known as the "Bill of Rights" and which guarantee important civil liberties.

Reading the plain text of the Constitution provides little information. For example, the Constitution prohibits "unreasonable searches and seizures" by the police. To understand concepts in the Constitution, it is necessary to look to the decisions of the U.S. Supreme Court, which has the ultimate authority in interpreting the meaning of the Constitution. For example, the U.S. Supreme Court's 2001 decision in *Kyllo v. United States* held that scanning the outside of a person's house using a heat sensor to determine whether the person is growing marijuana is an unreasonable search—if it is done without first getting a search warrant from a judge. Each state also has its own constitution and a supreme court that is the ultimate authority on its meaning.

Also important are the written laws, or "statutes," passed by the U.S. Congress and the individual state legislatures. As with constitutional provisions, the U.S. Supreme Court and the state supreme courts are the ultimate authorities in interpreting the meaning of federal and state laws, respectively. However, the U.S. Supreme Court might find that a state law violates the U.S. Constitution, and a state supreme court might find that a state law violates either the state or U.S. Constitution.

Not every controversy reaches either the U.S. Supreme Court or the state supreme courts, however. Therefore, the decisions of other courts are also important. Trial courts hear evidence from both sides and make a decision, while appeals courts review the decisions made by trial courts. Sometimes rulings from appeals courts are appealed further to the U.S. Supreme Court or the state supreme courts.

Lawyers and courts refer to statutes and court decisions through a formal system of citations. Use of these citations reveals which court made the decision or which legislature passed the statute, and allows one to quickly locate the statute or court case online or in a law library. For example, the Supreme Court case *Brown v. Board of Education* has the legal citation 347 U.S. 483 (1954). At a law library, this 1954 decision can be found on page 483 of volume 347 of the U.S. Reports, which are the official collection of the Supreme Court's decisions. On the following page, you will find samples of all the major kinds of legal citation.

Finding sources of legal information on the Internet is relatively simple thanks to "portal" sites such as findlaw.com and lexisone.com, which allow the user to access a variety of constitutions, statutes, court opinions, law review articles, news articles, and other useful sources of information. For example, findlaw.com offers access to all Supreme Court decisions since 1893. Other useful sources of information include gpo.gov, which contains a complete copy of the U.S. Code, and thomas.loc.gov, which offers access to bills pending before Congress, as well as recently passed laws. Of course, the Internet changes every second of every day, so it is best to do some independent searching.

Of course, many people still do their research at law libraries, some of which are open to the public. For example, some state governments and universities offer the public access to their law collections. Law librarians can be of great assistance, as even experienced attorneys need help with legal research from time to time.

Common Citation Forms

Source of Law	Sample Citation	Notes
U.S. Supreme Court	*Employment Division v. Smith*, 485 U.S. 660 (1988)	The U.S. Reports is the official record of Supreme Court decisions. There is also an unofficial Supreme Court ("S. Ct.") reporter.
U.S. Court of Appeals	*United States v. Lambert*, 695 F.2d 536 (11th Cir. 1983)	Appellate cases appear in the Federal Reporter, designated by "F." The 11th Circuit has jurisdiction in Alabama, Florida, and Georgia.
U.S. District Court	*Carillon Importers, Ltd. v. Frank Pesce Group, Inc.*, 913 F.Supp. 1559 (S.D.Fla. 1996)	Federal trial-level decisions are reported in the Federal Supplement ("F. Supp."). Some states have multiple federal districts; this case originated in the Southern District of Florida.
U.S. Code	Thomas Jefferson Commemoration Commission Act, 36 U.S.C., §149 (2002)	Sometimes the popular names of legislation—names with which the public may be familiar—are included with the U.S. Code citation.
State Supreme Court	*Sterling v. Cupp*, 290 Ore. 611, 614, 625 P.2d 123, 126 (1981)	The Oregon Supreme Court decision is reported in both the state's reporter and the Pacific regional reporter.
State Statute	Pennsylvania Abortion Control Act of 1982, 18 Pa. Cons. Stat. 3203-3220 (1990)	States use many different citation formats for their statutes.

Cases and Statutes

Witherspoon v. Illinois, 391 U.S. 510, 516–17 (1968)
U.S. Supreme Court ruled that a court cannot exclude potential jurors simply for expressing general objections to capital punishment.

Furman v. Georgia, 408 U.S. 238 (1972)
U.S. Supreme Court created a moratorium on capital punishment in the United States by determining that the death sentences in the cases before the court represented cruel and unusual punishment in violation of the Eighth Amendment.

Gregg v. Georgia, 428 U.S. 153 (1976)
U.S. Supreme Court ruled that capital punishment does not violate the Eighth Amendment when the law sets clear standards that guide juries in deciding whether to impose the death penalty.

McCleskey v. Kemp, 481 U.S. 279 (1987)
U.S. Supreme Court examined a study showing that black defendants in Georgia were statistically more likely to be sentenced to death than white defendants, and ruled that the study results did not invalidate Georgia's death penalty statute because the statistics did not establish a violation of any specific defendant's constitutional rights.

Payne v. Tennessee, 501 U.S. 808 (1991)
U.S. Supreme Court overruled its earlier decision *Booth v. Maryland,* 482 U.S. 496 (1987), and held that the use of victim impact statements is permissible to counteract a defendant's introduction of character evidence.

Dawson v. Delaware, 503 U.S. 159 (1992)
U.S. Supreme Court ruled that introducing evidence at a capital trial of a defendant's membership in a racist gang unfairly influenced the jury and therefore violated the defendant's constitutional right to due process of law.

Frye v. Lee, 235 F.3d 897 (4th Cir. 2000)
Federal appeals court ruled that despite the defense lawyer's heavy drinking during the time period of the trial, the defendant's death sentence was upheld due to lack of specific evidence that the lawyer failed to represent the defendant effectively.

Bell v. Cone, 535 U.S. 685 (2002)
U.S. Supreme Court upheld death sentence (for murders committed in 1980) of a Vietnam veteran whose lawyer did not call any witnesses or give a closing argument during the sentencing phase of the trial to support the defendant's claims of post-traumatic stress disorder (PTSD) and drug abuse.

Atkins v. Virginia, 536 U.S. 304 (2002)
U.S. Supreme Court held that executing people who are mentally retarded is cruel and unusual punishment in violation of the Eighth Amendment.

Hughes v. Mississippi, 892 So.2d 2003 (Miss. 2004)
State supreme court held that a capital defendant is not entitled to an evidentiary hearing on the issue of whether he is mentally retarded.

Roper v. Simmons, 543 U.S. 551 (2005)
U.S. Supreme Court ruled that people cannot be executed for crimes they committed before they turned 18.

Bell v. Cone, 543 U.S. 447 (2005) (**per curiam**)
U.S. Supreme Court again upheld the death penalty of Gary Cone, finding that a law imposing the death penalty for "especially heinous, atrocious, or cruel" murders was not vague.

USA Patriot Reauthorization Act of 2005
Imposed time limits on habeas corpus proceedings in federal courts.

Myers v. Oklahoma, 130 P.3d 262 (**Okl. Cr. 2005**)
State court rejected claim of mental retardation by capital defendant.

Cone v. Bell, No. 99–5279 (**6th Cir., June 19, 2007**)
Federal appeals court rejected additional habeas corpus appeals by Gary Cone.

Panetti v. Quarterman, 551 U.S. ___ (2007)
U.S. Supreme Court ruled that a man who had schizophrenia and defended himself at trial while wearing a cowboy outfit could not be executed unless the lower court found that he understood the reason for his execution.

Terms and Concepts

habeas corpus
ineffective assistance of counsel
retribution
deterrence
cruel and unusual punishment
victim impact statement
victims' rights laws
eye for an eye
death qualification

Introduction: What Is Capital Punishment?

1 Harry Henderson, *Capital Punishment* (New York: Facts on File, 2000), 6.
2 U.S. Const. amend. VIII.
3 Jason DeParle, "Willie Going to Chair as Proud Man," *New Orleans Times-Picayune*, December 27, 1984.
4 Helen Prejean, *Dead Man Walking* (New York: Random House, 1993), 128.
5 *Ibid.*, 210–211.
6 *Ibid.*, 213.
7 Jason DeParle, "Victim's Parents Watch Willie Die," *New Orleans Times-Picayune*, December 28, 1984.
8 Prejean, *Dead Man Walking*, 213.
9 Jesse Jackson, *Legal Lynching: Racism, Injustice & the Death Penalty* (New York: Marlowe & Co., 1996), 57.
10 Exodus, 21: 23–24.
11 Exodus, 21: 32.
12 Pope John Paul II, *Evangelium Vitae*, Encyclical Letter, March 25, 1995.

Point: The Death Penalty Is an Effective Deterrent to Crime

1 *Gregg v. Georgia*, 428 U.S. 153, 185 (1976) (plurality opinion).
2 See Justice for All: A Criminal Justice Reform Organization. Available online. URL: http://www.jfa.net/deathpenalty.html. Accessed November 14, 2007.
3 Cass R. Sunstein and Adrian Vermeule, "Is Capital Punishment Morally Required? Acts, Omissions, and Life-Life Tradeoffs," *Stanford Law Review* 58 (2005): 706.
4 *Ibid.*, 707
5 Charles N. W. Keckler, "Life v. Death: Who Should Capital Punishment Marginally Deter?" *Journal of Law, Economics & Policy* 2 (2006): 149.
6 Isaac Ehrlich, "The Deterrent Effect of Capital Punishment—A Question of Life and Death," *American Economic Review* 65, no. 3 (June 1975): 397–417.
7 Hashem Dezhbakhsh, Paul H. Rubin, Joanna M. Shepherd, "Does Capital Punishment Have a Deterrent Effect? New Evidence from Postmoratorium Panel Data (abstract)," *American Law and Economics Review* 5, no. 2 (August 2003): 344–376.

8 H. Naci Mocan and R. Kaj Gittings, "Getting off Death Row: Commuted Sentences and the Deterrent Effect of Capital Punishment (abstract)," *Journal of Law and Economics*, 46 (2003): 453–478.
9 Paul R. Zimmerman, "State Executions, Deterrence, and the Incidence of Murder," *Journal of Applied Economics* 7, no. 1 (May 2004): 163–193.
10 Paul R. Zimmerman, "Estimates of the Deterrent Effect of Alternative Execution Methods in the United States: 1978–2000," *American Journal of Economics and Sociology* 65, no. 4 (October 2006): 909–941.
11 *Furman v. Georgia*, 408 U.S. 238, 253 (1972) (Douglas, J., concurring).
12 Frank G. Carrington, as cited in Alan I. Bigel, *Justices William J. Brennan, Jr. and Thurgood Marshall on Capital Punishment: Its Constitutionality, Morality, Deterrent Effect, and Interpretation by the Court* (New York: University Press of America, 1997), 44.
13 Arlen Specter, "A Swifter Death Penalty Would Be an Effective Deterrent," in *Does Capital Punishment Deter Crime*, ed. Stephen E. Schonebaum (San Diego: Greenhaven Press, 1998). First published in *Human Events*, July 15, 1995.
14 Sunstein and Vermeule, "Is Capital Punishment Morally Required," 716.

Counterpoint: The Death Penalty Is Not an Effective Deterrent to Crime

1 *Gregg v. Georgia*, 428 U.S. 153, 235–36 (1976) (Marshall, J., dissenting).
2 *Ibid.*
3 *Ibid.*
4 Jeffrey Fagan, "Public Policy Choices on Deterrence and the Death Penalty: A Critical Review of New Evidence," testimony before the Joint Committee on the Judiciary of the Massachusetts Legislature, July 14, 2005.
5 Jackson, *Legal Lynching*, 124.
6 Richard Rhodes, *Why They Kill: The Discoveries of a Maverick Criminologist* (New York: Alfred A. Knopf, 1999), 88–89.
7 Michael Kronenwetter, *Capital Punishment: A Reference Handbook* (Santa Barbara, CA: ABL-CLIO, 2001), 27.

8 Shirley Dicks, ed., *Congregation of the Condemned: Voices Against the Death Penalty* (Buffalo, NY: Prometheus Books, 1991), 75.

9 *Bell v. Cone*, 535 U.S. 685 (2002).

10 Dicks, *Congregation of the Condemned*, 77.

11 *Atkins v. Virginia*, 536 U.S. 304 (2002).

12 Joanna M. Shepherd, "Deterrence versus Brutalization: Capital Punishment's Differing Impact among States," *Michigan Law Review* 104 (November 2005): 248.

13 Kronenwetter, *Capital Punishment*, 31.

14 *Ibid.*, 33.

Point: Reducing Limits on Capital Punishment Would Make It More Effective

1 Cass R. Sunstein and Adrian Vermeule, "Deterring Murder: A Reply," *Stanford Law Review* 58 (December 2005): 848–849.

2 Richard C. Dieter, "Millions Misspent: What Politicians Don't Say About the High Costs of the Death Penalty," in *The Death Penalty in America: Current Controversies*, ed. Hugo A. Bedau (New York: Oxford University Press, 1997), 407.

3 *Ibid.*, 402.

4 Alex Kozinski and Sean Gallagher, "The Death Penalty Can Be Economically Effective," in *The Death Penalty: Opposing Viewpoints*, ed. Paul A. Winters (San Diego: Greenhaven Press, 1997). First published as "For an Honest Death Penalty," *New York Times*, March 8, 1995.

5 *Dawson v. Delaware*, 503 U.S. 159, 162–63, 166 (1992).

6 *Dawson v. Delaware*, 503 U.S. 159, 170, 174–75 (1992) (Thomas, J., dissenting).

7 Joanna M. Shepherd, "Murders of Passion, Execution Delays, and the Deterrence of Capital Punishment (abstract)," *Journal of Legal Studies* 33 (June 2004): 283–322.

8 Shepherd, "Deterrence versus Brutalization," 233–234.

9 Shepherd, "Murders of Passion (abstract)."

10 *Bell v. Cone*, 535 U.S. 685 (2002).

11 *Cone v. Bell*, 359 F. 3d 785 (2004).

12 *Bell v. Cone*, 543 U.S. 447 (2005) (per curiam).

13 *Cone v. Bell*, No. 99–5279 (6th Cir., June 19, 2007).

Counterpoint: It Is Too Easy to Convict and Execute People

1 *Booth v. Maryland*, 482 U.S. 496, 499–500 (1987).

2 *Booth v. Maryland*, 482 U.S. 496, 508 (1987).

3 *Payne v. Tennessee*, 501 U.S. 808, 859–60 (1991) (Stevens, J., dissenting).

4 *Witherspoon v. Illinois*, 391 U.S. 510, 516–17 (1968).

5 *Witherspoon v. Illinois*, 391 U.S. 510, 517 (1968).

6 Clay S. Conrad, "Are You 'Death Qualified'?" *Cato Institute Daily Dispatch*, August 10, 2000. Available online. URL: www.cato.org.

7 Michael L. Radelet, Hugo Adam Bedau, and Constance L. Putnam, *In Spite of Innocence: Erroneous Convictions in Capital* Cases (Boston: Northeastern University Press, 1992), 121.

8 Jackson, *Legal Lynching*, 62.

Point: Capital Punishment Is Applied Fairly in Our Society

1 *McCleskey v. Kemp*, 481 U.S. 279, 306 (1987).

2 Ernest Van Den Haag, "The Death Penalty Once More," in *The Death Penalty in America: Current Controversies*, ed. Hugo Adam Bedau (New York: Oxford University Press, 1997), 449.

3 *McClesky v. Kemp*, 481 U.S. 279, 311 (1987).

4 Criminal Justice Legal Foundation, press release, September 24, 2001.

5 *Atkins v. Virginia*, 536 U.S. 304 (2002) (Scalia, A., dissenting).

6 *Ibid.*

7 *Myers v. Oklahoma*, 130 P.3d 262 (Okl. Cr. 2005).

8 Dora W. Klein, "Categorical Exclusions from Capital Punishment: How Many Wrongs Make a Right?" *Brooklyn Law Review* 72, no. 4 (2005): 1221.

9 *Ibid.*, 1228.

10 *Ford v. Wainwright*, 477 U.S. 399 (1986).

11 American Bar Association, Policy Recommendation 122A, August 8, 2006.

12 Laurie T. Izutsu, "Applying *Atkins v. Virginia* to Defendants with Severe Mental

Illness," *Brooklyn Law Review* 72, no. 4 (2005): 998.

13 *Panetti v. Quarterman*, 551 U.S. ___ (2007), brief for petitioner.

14 *Ibid.*

15 *Panetti v. Quarterman*, 551 U.S. ___ (2007).

16 *Ibid.*

17 *Ibid.*

18 *Ibid.*

19 Quoted in Ralph Blumenthal, "Supreme Court Blocks Execution of Delusional Killer," *New York Times*, June 29, 2007.

Counterpoint: Capital Punishment Is Applied Unfairly in Our Society

1 Richard C. Dieter, *The Death Penalty in Black & White: Who Lives, Who Dies, Who Decides* (Washington, D.C.: Death Penalty Information Center, 1998).

2 *Ibid.*

3 *McCleskey v. Kemp*, 481 U.S. 279, 367 (1987) (Stevens, J., dissenting).

4 Hugo Adam Bedau, "The Case Against the Death Penalty." Available online. URL: www.aclu.org.

5 American Civil Liberties Union, *Briefing Paper: The Death Penalty*, no. 14 (Spring 1999): 1.

6 *Ibid.*

7 *Frye v. Lee*, 235 F.3d 897 (4th Cir. 2000).

8 *Ibid.*

9 *Ibid.*

10 *Atkins v. Virginia*, 536 U.S. 304 (2002).

11 *Ibid.*

12 *Ibid.*

13 *Roper v. Simmons*, 543 U.S. 551 (2005).

14 Richard C. Dieter, *On the Front Line: Law Enforcement Views on the Death Penalty* (Washington, D.C.: Death Penalty Information Center, 1995).

15 *Hughes v. Mississippi*, 892 So.2d 203 (Miss. 2004).

16 *Ibid.*

17 *Ibid.*

18 Ernie Poortinga and Melvin Guyer, "Quantum of Evidence of Mental Retardation Required of a Defendant in Application Seeking Postconviction Relief," *Journal of the American Academy of Psychiatry and Law* 34, no. 1 (2006): 114.

19 *Ibid.*

20 American Civil Liberties Union Capital Punishment Project, *How the Death Penalty Weakens U.S. International Interests* (New York: ACLU National Office, 2004), 5.

21 *Panetti v. Quarterman*, 551 U.S. ___ (2007).

22 The Justice Project, press release, "U.S. Supreme Court Says that Texas may not Execute Severely Mentally Ill Man," June 28, 2007.

23 Izutsu, "Applying *Atkins*," 1021.

24 *Ibid.*

Bigel, Alan I. *Justices William J. Brennan, Jr. and Thurgood Marshall on Capital Punishment: Its Constitutionality, Morality, Deterrent Effect, and Interpretation by the Court.* New York: University Press of America, 1997.

Henderson, Harry. *Capital Punishment.* New York: Facts on File, 2000.

Kronenwetter, Michael. *Capital Punishment: A Reference Handbook.* Santa Barbara, Calif.: ABL-CLIO, 2001.

Rhodes, Richard. *Why They Kill: The Discoveries of a Maverick Criminologist.* New York: Alfred A. Knopf, 1999.

Shepherd, Joanna M. "Deterrence versus Brutalization: Capital Punishment's Differing Impact among States." *Michigan Law Review* 104 (November 2005): 203–255

Wolf, Robert V. *Capital Punishment.* Philadelphia: Chelsea House Publishers, 1997.

Pro–Capital Punishment

Ehrlich, Issac. "The Deterrent Effect of Capital Punishment—A Question of Life and Death." *American Economic Review* 65, no. 3 (June 1975): 397–417.

Charles N. W. Keckler, "Life v. Death: Who Should Capital Punishment Marginally Deter?" *Journal of Law, Economics & Policy* 2 (2006): 101–161.

Kozinski, Alex, and Sean Gallagher. "The Death Penalty Can Be Economically Effective." In *The Death Penalty: Opposing Viewpoints,* edited by Paul A. Winters. San Diego: Greenhaven Press, 1997.

Specter, Arlen. "A Swifter Death Penalty Would Be an Effective Deterrent." In *Does Capital Punishment Deter Crime?*, edited by Stephen E. Schonebaum, 17–21. San Diego: Greenhaven Press, 1998.

Sunstein, Cass R., and Adrian Vermeule. "Is Capital Punishment Morally Required? Acts, Omissions, and Life-Life Tradeoffs." *Stanford Law Review* 58 (2005): 703–750.

Van Den Haag, Ernest. "The Death Penalty Once More." In *The Death Penalty in America: Current Controversies,* edited by Hugo Adam Bedau, 445–456. New York: Oxford University Press, 1997.

Anti–Capital Punishment

American Civil Liberties Union Capital Punishment Project. *How the Death Penalty Weakens U.S. International Interests.* New York: ACLU National Office, 2004.

Dicks, Shirley, ed. *Congregation of the Condemned: Voices Against the Death Penalty.* Buffalo, N.Y.: Prometheus Books, 1991.

Dieter, Richard C. "Millions Misspent: What Politicians Don't Say About the High Costs of the Death Penalty." In *The Death Penalty in America: Current Controversies,* edited by Hugo A. Bedau, 401–413. New York: Oxford University Press, 1997.

Dieter, Richard C. *On the Front Line: Law Enforcement Views on the Death Penalty.* Washington, D.C.: Death Penalty Information Center, 1995.

Dieter, Richard C. *The Death Penalty in Black & White: Who Lives, Who Dies, Who Decides.* Washington, D.C.: Death Penalty Information Center, 1998.

Jackson, Jesse. *Legal Lynching: Racism, Injustice & the Death Penalty.* New York: Marlowe & Co., 1996.

Prejean, Helen. *Dead Man Walking.* New York: Random House, 1993.

Radelet, Michael L., Hugo Adam Bedau, and Constance L. Putnam. *In Spite of Innocence: Erroneous Convictions in Capital Cases.* Boston: Northeastern University Press, 1992.

Web Sites

American Civil Liberties Union
http://www.aclu.org
National organization defending individual rights such as free speech, freedom of choice in abortion, and rights in the criminal justice system. Practical information about working to abolish the death penalty.

Amnesty International
http://www.amnesty.org
International human rights organization advocating for the abolition of the death penalty worldwide. Extensive information about the death penalty, including international comparisons.

RESOURCES ///// ▷

Criminal Justice Legal Foundation

http://www.cjlf.org

Nonprofit legal organization supporting victims' rights and swift justice over excessive protections for the criminally accused. Information and legal arguments about current cases.

Death Penalty Information Center

http://www.deathpenaltyinfo.org

Nonprofit organization that educates the public and the media about anti-death penalty viewpoints. In-depth reports and information about current cases.

Justice For All

www.prodeathpenalty.com and www.jfa.net

Organization advocating for criminal justice reform to protect innocent people's lives and property. Information about scheduled executions and an extensive collection of essays and articles.

National Coalition to Abolish the Death Penalty

http://www.ncadp.org

National organization working to abolish the death penalty through legal and legislative advocacy at the local, state, and federal levels. Concise fact sheets and statistics about executions.

Washington Legal Foundation

www.wlf.org

Nonprofit legal organization advocating for various conservative causes, including military defense, business rights, and criminal justice reform. Plainly written summaries of recent litigation.

PICTURE CREDITS

PAGE

15: AP Images/Mel Evans
24: AP Images/AF
33: AP Images/Carrie Osgood, AF
69: AP Images/Sangjib Min
90: AP Images/AF

COVER

Glenn R. McGloughlin/Shutterstock.com

INDEX ||||▷

ALAN MARZILLI, M.A., J.D., lives in Washington, D.C., and is a program associate with Advocates for Human Potential, Inc., a research and consulting firm based in Sudbury, Massachusetts, and Albany, New York. He primarily works on developing training and educational materials for agencies of the federal government on topics such as housing, mental health policy, employment, and transportation. He has spoken on mental health issues in 30 states, the District of Columbia, and Puerto Rico; his work has included training mental health administrators, nonprofit management and staff, and people with mental illnesses and their families on a wide variety of topics, including effective advocacy, community-based mental health services, and housing. Marzilli has written several handbooks and training curricula that are used nationally and as far away as the U.S. territory of Guam. Additionally, he managed statewide and national mental health advocacy programs and worked for several public interest lobbying organizations while studying law at Georgetown University. Marzilli has written more than a dozen books, including numerous titles in the *Point/Counterpoint* series.

14, 34